The Historical Roots of the ANC

edited by
Ben Turok

JACANA

*Grateful acknowledgements are due to the
Mayibuye Centre at the University of the Western Cape
for permission to use the photographs included in this book.
Thanks are also due to Aneesah Reynolds, who transcribed at great
speed the oral presentations on which this book is based; to Vaun
Cornell, who admirably edited the transcriptions; to Axel Schmidt of
the Friedrich-Ebert-Stiftung, who assisted with funding; to the office
of the ANC Chief Whip; to the ANC Parliamentary Committee on
Political Education, which hosted the presentations; and to all the
ANC comrades who helped to design the theoretical
framework of the series.*

First published by Jacana Media (Pty) Ltd in 2010

10 Orange Street
Sunnyside
Auckland Park 2092
South Africa
+2711 628 3200
www.jacana.co.za

ISBN 978-1-77009-965-4

Set in Ehrhardt 12/16pt
Printed and bound by Ultra Litho (Pty) Limited, Johannesburg
Job No. 001345

See a complete list of Jacana titles at www.jacana.co.za

*To Moses Kotane, a wise and highly intellectual
leader of the African National Congress
and South African Communist Party,
this volume is dedicated.*

Contents

Introduction
Ben Turok

Two themes dominate twentieth-century history: the struggle of the colonised peoples of Asia, Africa and the Caribbean to free themselves from colonial domination; and the struggle of working people either to achieve a social revolution and build post-capitalist societies or to radically redistribute social wealth within the capitalist framework.

These themes find an extraordinary resonance in the history of the African National Congress. Apart from its longevity (it is due to celebrate its centenary in 2012), the ANC evolved in a racially and culturally diverse society with a complex history where the issues of colonial conquest and class exploitation were intermeshed. This book attempts to capture the complexity of that history as a contribution to a better understanding of our present conjuncture.

The contents of this book are the result of a series of lectures delivered to the ANC Parliamentary Caucus during 2010 by leading figures in the ANC. The lectures set out the origins of the ANC as a movement that evolved through struggle, its political doctrine and

1

policies, and the different phases through which the movement passed to the present, when it is the ruling party in South Africa.

The liberation movement was forged during a period of European conquest and colonial occupation that gave birth to new social and political forces. Initially pursuing ethnically and racially specific agendas, Africans, Coloureds and Indians established distinct political formations during that period, laying the basis for what became a formal organisation of Africans in 1912.

The chapters analyse the emergence of the basic institutions of national oppression, class exploitation and gender discrimination that underpin the system characterised as colonialism of a special type in the modern period. These institutions arose from the conquest of the African people and the dispossession of their land and its wealth and the importation of Asian slave and indentured labour well into the twentieth century.

From the mid-seventeenth century South Africa evolved as a white settler colony. After the Anglo–Boer War, which brought the region under British rule, an explicit monopoly over political power was exercised by the white minority, undergirding the economic power of white mining, agrarian and industrial capital. That power was further buttressed by special bodies of law applicable to the colonial subjects. After the formation of the Union of South Africa in 1910, black South

Africans were governed as conquered, colonial peoples who could claim no rights.

The key institutions of national oppression, class exploitation and gender discrimination were elaborated through wars of conquest and legislation between 1867 and 1910. The changes they wrought transformed what had until then been two mutually dependent yet distinct societies, into a single socio-economic unit. Opposition to the social and political order that emerged consequently embraced:

1 an anti-colonial dimension derived from the primary and secondary phases of resistance, merged with the twentieth-century tri-continental movement for colonial freedom;

2 a democratic political thrust inspired in part by a Christian humanism and by secular democratic principles; and

3 a revolutionary socialist tradition, derived from the left wing of the labour movement, that sought to address the economic exploitation of the working classes.

At its formation in 1912 the ANC's vision was based on the principle of African unity and self-determination in response to white unity embodied in the Act of Union of 1909. But the period prior to Union, though often glossed over in our history, remains important for understanding the various threads drawn together in the ANC. Apart from the last wars of resistance, the late nineteenth century witnessed modern political struggles conducted by new African political associations through various newspapers, the Christian church and its derivative, Ethiopianism.

The first decade of the twentieth century witnessed the founding of political bodies, such as the African People's Organisation (APO), the anti-poll tax uprising in Natal (the Bambatha Rebellion) and the first general strike by black workers, when Indian canefield and coal mineworkers struck in 1907. Agitation to oppose the colour bar clauses in the Constitution of the proposed Union also reached a climax.

A pan-African vision, inspired by Pixley Seme, animated the ANC of 1912 and instigated the formation of like-named bodies in virtually all the British colonies of southern Africa. Then came the First World War, whose impact resulted in the Russian Revolution of 1917, the collapse of Europe's land-based empires and the invocation of the principle of national self-determination in the ordering of world affairs. Anti-colonialism and anti-imperialism throughout the Third World were greatly stimulated by these developments.

The ANC emerged as a political movement of African modernists who sought to employ the institutions of colonial domination and government for the redress of a number of national grievances and disabilities. As people who regarded themselves as loyal subjects, the tone and tenor of their petitions and appeals to white authority urging equality before the law and political rights within the existing political order were moderate and measured. But the movement absorbed other influences from the cosmopolitan environment in which it operated.

Individually and severally, the different ethnic organisations – African, Indian and Coloured – came to realise that common action, in pursuit of shared goals, would enhance their capacity. Through united political action, the South African liberation struggle gradually brought together a united front of the African, Indian and Coloured people – the oppressed black majority – and harnessed the energies of white democrats, to constitute the Congress Alliance. The adherence of the leading black trade union federation, the South African Congress of Trade Unions, to the alliance in 1955 drew together the principal strands of opposition to national oppression. The Congress Alliance then consisted of the African National Congress, the South African Indian Congress, the South African Coloured People's Organisation, the South African Congress of Democrats and the South African Congress of Trade Unions. Unity was ensured by meetings of the joint executives and by a secretariat consisting of representatives of each of the component organisations, who met frequently, often under clandestine conditions. While membership of each was based on race, there was a great deal of unity in action. The ANC opened its ranks to all races when Umkhonto we Sizwe (MK) was formed and more broadly in exile. This was confirmed when the ANC was re-established openly in South Africa in 1990.

The South African liberation struggle became an example of a successful and mutually beneficial relationship among the national, labour and communist movements in a country at the crossroads between East and West, on a continent in the throes of a fierce struggle for independence and national freedom.

Given South Africa's geo-political significance, the South African liberation movement necessarily developed an international perspective. From the late nineteenth century, black political leaders had cultivated international networks amongst sympathetic institutions, bodies and individuals in Britain and other parts of Europe. Black students attending colleges and universities abroad established links with those of other colonies; black clerics used their churches to network with the African Methodist Episcopal (AME) Church in the United States; while black educationists built close ties with their American and Caribbean counterparts. Through the pan-African movement political leaders firmed up links with other African movements on the continent and in the diaspora. Such links enabled the movement to borrow freely from movements in other parts of the world, including those in Europe. Its anti-racism was complemented by the anti-imperialist ethic of Third World liberation movements, in particular Afro-Asian and pan-African solidarity.

In general terms, the liberation movement initially identified with and supported the cause of liberal democracy in South Africa and in the world. The delegation it sent to the Pan-African Congress in Paris in 1921 encountered a large network of other colonial liberation movements at the meeting. Appreciation that South Africa's position was neither unique nor unusual fostered an ethic of solidarity and underscored the need to create a united front of all the oppressed in South Africa.

The South African environment, where gender and national oppression were intertwined with class exploitation, led to the organic coalescence of these three currents around a common programme – the Freedom Charter, which remains the centre of the movement's policy.

The movement inspired by Karl Marx during the nineteenth century and shaped by *The Communist Manifesto* declared its opposition to colonialism, imperialism and systems of racial domination. Marxism arrived on our shores with the white workers who flocked to this country in droves after the discovery of gold. East European artisans and intellectuals, fleeing religious intolerance and persecution, also arrived in South Africa imbued with socialist ideas. The South African labour movement was initially based on the struggles of the trade unions of skilled whites on the mines and related industries, but it soon drew in the unskilled black workers and was compelled to respond to the living experience of black labour.

Labour reformism in Britain and other parts of Europe had evolved at the expense of the semi-skilled and unskilled workers. In South Africa, where these sectors of the labouring classes usually coincided with race, labour reformism took on a racist tone. This found expression in the policies of the South African Labour Party, whose programme called for the exclusion of blacks from the urban areas or else their restriction to low-paid, unskilled work.

The revolution in Russia during 1917 had a ripple effect throughout the world, and South Africa was no exception. The Bolshevik victory of November 1917 reaffirmed anti-colonialism and anti-racism as key components of the Marxist programme in addition to awakening class consciousness among all South African workers. The Communist Party of South Africa (CPSA), formed in 1921 by the white working-class leaders who refused to support the war in 1914, made slow headway, since it was preoccupied with winning support among the white workers. The racist rhetoric and policies of whites who called themselves socialists made it difficult for the CPSA to root itself in the African working class. It took several decades before Marxism became a widely accepted ideology in the working class and for the ANC willingly to accept communists as committed participants in the liberation struggle.

Marxism understood the system of racial oppression as a function of capitalism that developed in a colonial context. It espoused a theory centred on the class struggle as the motor of history. From that perspective, the South African system of colonialism of a special type was one variant of an international system of imperialist domination in which the colonial power and the colonised lived within the same country. After a decade of wrestling with the peculiarities of the local environment, South African Marxists came to accept that the class struggle would proceed through and in tandem with the national struggle against colonial domination.

Marxism–Leninism introduced the notion of a vanguard party, an organisation of revolutionary cadres equipped with the theory and practice of revolution. It contended that the revolution to overthrow the capitalist order would be made and led by the working class itself. The experience of the Russian Revolution had demonstrated that in order to succeed, the working class would have to offer leadership to other classes, class fractions and strata that opposed an oppressive order through class alliances and coalitions. In colonial and semi-colonial countries, such alliances required cooperation with the movement for freedom and independence. Marxism, in all its fractious history in South Africa and elsewhere, was distinguished from both labour reformism and social democracy by its commitment to the national liberation struggle and consistent opposition to racism.

By working in temporary and long-term alliances with Marxists, the ANC incorporated many of their ideas into its thinking, even though with considerable variation. Historically, there has been little friction between the Marxist conception of the ANC as an alliance of a variety of class forces and the movement's self-perception as the principal vehicle of national liberation.

Parliamentary democracy, human rights, the rule of law, regular multi-party elections and social justice have been amongst the ANC's core values from its inauguration. As a movement comprising in the main the working people of the cities and the rural poor, the ANC took on board many of the ideas associated with the more progressive practices in social democracy. This was particularly so after the Second World War, during which the movement adopted 'Africans' Claims' in 1943 as its programmatic statement, anticipating many of the features of the Universal Declaration of Human Rights of 1948.

After 1943 the separation of powers, the secular state, protection and respect for minorities, and accountable and transparent government became central to the ANC's value system. In pursuit of some of these, the ANC in government after 1994 has instituted a welfare system that offers protection to the most vulnerable members of society. Civil society has also been allocated a significant role in the movement's vision.

The chapters in this volume elaborate on all these influences. The original presentations to the ANC Parliamentary Caucus were taped, transcribed and edited.

What is important is that the reader appreciate the diversity of influences on the ANC, indicative of a living, breathing and growing movement that is sensitive to both the national and international environments in which it operates. However, in the end, the ANC remains true to its origins and history even before it was formalised as an organisation. It remains committed to the total liberation of the African people and the other historically oppressed peoples and to the pursuit of a non-racial, non-sexist democratic society in which all can live in harmony.

SOCIAL ORIGINS

Kgalema Motlanthe & Z. Pallo Jordan

Kgalema Motlanthe

I have been asked to deal with the history that preceded the formation of the African National Congress. I thought about this a great deal and came to the view that perhaps what is really needed is to give a brief outline of what was common in society in general, worldwide, at the time. In this way we will be able to deal with basic concepts and therefore understand the context within which the ANC came into being.

All human beings, all living organisms, have to derive the means to support life from nature. The air you breathe, the water you drink, the food you eat in order to support life: nature provides all of this, but it does not deliver it to you in a canister, bottle or little tub. You can lie in the shade of a paw paw tree and when the paw paw ripens it will fall on you, but you still have to take the paw paw and put it in your mouth. That is necessary labour: by just this simple act you are producing the means to support life. This is our starting point – common to all living beings, including human beings – the performance of necessary labour.

Now, as members of the animal kingdom we have access to all that nature offers, free and unfettered. There are no restrictions: you can walk to the river at any time in order to get water. So there is no problem in terms of how you relate to nature at that level. There is perfect harmony between you and nature. All the same, as you perform this necessary labour of walking to the river and drawing water, the human body exposes its own limitations. It is possible for instance that you begin by picking low-lying fruits but once these are exhausted, the ripe ones remaining are on high branches, completely beyond your reach. To get at them, you would use a stick perhaps. And so, almost immediately a contradiction arises between you and nature. You have to *act* on nature in order to produce the means to support life. Once you reach your body's limitations, you can pick up a stick to extend your body. That stick is called an instrument of production because it is an extension of the human body; it helps you to produce the means to support life. All subsequent technological products are simply an extension of the human body.

In the past a community would have access to the land for tilling or pasturage, to forests for hunting and rivers and springs for water. No restriction is imposed by anybody. What you produce in order to support life is owned by you as a community because you all have equal access – to the river, the forest, the land. As a community you lead a communal life because the means of production are owned communally. This also determines not only how you produce and distribute the means to support life but the very nature of society. When you cultivate the land, you have to settle in order to plant, wait for the crops to grow and then harvest them, whereas societies that exist by hunting and gathering are nomadic.

A problem will arise once somebody, or some section of a population, claims that the river or forest or field belongs to them to the exclusion of others. Now the rest of the community needs permission to draw water or hunt or till. This is the law of property and it has several consequences. How does the owner enforce his claim and what does this force consist of?

This claim to property would not even arise as long as the level of development of the instruments of production remains primitive. If, for example, it takes a whole day to catch a rabbit, which is consumed in one meal, I am forced to go out every day and hunt. My capacity to produce the means to support life is so low that I have to continue producing all the time in order to survive. I have no time to do anything else. As long as production is at subsistence level – as long as you are unable to produce enough to free you at least partially from this necessary labour – there is no accumulation.

It is only once human beings are capable of producing more than they need for survival that the concept of accumulation arises – this is the function of the instruments of production and the ability of human beings to use those instruments to produce more. Once society has reached this stage, and only then, some members can live without the burden of performing necessary labour. This creates the possibility for some individuals in the community to lay claim to a particular river, or field or forest, as belonging to them, to the exclusion of others, because certain others can be released from producing the means to support life and tasked to guard the river.

At this point the relations between members of the community and between the members and the means of production become more complex. Those who claim ownership of a river or field or forest as their property and those who are excluded from ownership form two very different classes: the propertied and the propertyless. This is where classes arise in society for the first time.

The previously communal community is now divided into classes: those who own the means of production and those who do not. Typically, the society that succeeded the communal form of society was a slave society, where those who owned the means of production also owned the labour power of slaves. Slaves were owned as property, the way you would own a horse or a pair of shoes. They had absolutely no life outside that relationship to the slave owners. The best textbook on slavery I can refer you to is the Old Testament; it will tell you much about slavery as a mode of production.

To determine the phases of society's development, we need to be guided by what is called the mode of production. The combination of the forces of production – the instruments of production together with the people who use those instruments – and the relations of production (above all, property relations) gives the mode of production. By mode of production we mean the way society produces the means to support life and the way these means are exchanged in society. In communal society the mode of production is very simple: everybody has equal and free access to all the means of production, and the property relations are communal. The mode of production, which is really the economic structure of society, is the foundation that gives rise to ideas, ideology and politics: what is called the superstructure. The mode of production is what gives character to any social formation.

In the era of slavery, society consisted of two basic classes – the slave owners and the slaves. Slave owners were free from performing necessary labour; they could live off the production of others and delegate virtually every task to their slaves. What brought this era to an end was not the actions of the slaves to free themselves from their harsh existence. It was the development of the forces of production which came into conflict with the property relations.

Let me illustrate this by way of an example of an egg. If you take the shell of the egg as depicting property relations or relations of production, then inside that shell, out of the yoke, an embryo develops. While developing, the embryo needs the shell – the shell is a condition for the embryo's further growth and development. So the relations of production at one point serve as necessary conditions for the further growth and development of the forces of production. During this stage religion will say that to crack the shell is a cardinal sin; poets and musicians will sing that there is perfect harmony between the embryo and the shell; while the laws will say that this is how things are destined to be and anybody who tampers with the arrangement is committing an offence. All of these depictions and interpretations are presented as the truth, and must be accepted as such. Factually, this is correct. The shell is a necessary protection for the further growth and development of this embryo and the embryo will get its nutrients from within the shell; therefore the shell is absolutely necessary, just as property relations are absolutely necessary.

So the mode of production under slavery is a necessary condition for the further growth and development of the forces of production until such time as these forces of production can no longer develop any further within the shell of slave property relations. Once that point is reached, there begins a period of social upheaval because the forces of production have to free themselves in the same way as the embryo must. It has to crack open the shell in order to develop and grow further under different conditions, under different property relations. It takes centuries, but this is how society evolves and moves forward: from the era of slavery to that of feudalism and then into the modern capitalist society in which society is basically divided into the two classes of capitalists and workers.

◯◯◯

It was in the early stages of capitalism that Europe first made contact with southern Africa. Jan van Riebeeck was sent out to the Cape in 1652 by the world's first multinational, joint-stock company, the Dutch East India Company, which had a trading network and a series of trading stations and establishments all over the Indian Ocean world. At that point the natives in this part of Africa had not experienced the division of society into classes. The predominant mode of production was still based on communal ownership of the means of production and the dominant ideas in society, its value system, were those of a communal society. When the two societies met – Dutch and Khoikhoi and, a bit later, Dutch and Xhosa – there was a clash of cultures and ideologies. The indigenous people, who were still part of a communal society, were dragged into the stage of capitalism without experiencing any of the intervening phases through which Europe had passed. That is why some of the values and habits of a communal society are still retained by people, particularly in the rural villages of South Africa. If, for instance, you are a youngster herding cattle and you allow them to wander into someone else's mealie fields, any parent or elder member of the community has the right to punish you. Again, if someone is orphaned, the community takes responsibility for his or her upkeep. And when people from the rural areas come to town and board a bus, children will know that they cannot remain seated if there is an elderly person standing. The value system under capitalism in the urban areas is different. Children will tell you that they have paid for their seat and have a right to sit on it. In the rural areas, moreover, the pace of life is much slower and people take their time to greet others properly and go through all the formalities and rituals. In the towns, the tempo is that of the clock: the hands keep moving all the time because that is how time is regulated in the modern world.

So the first encounter between Europeans and the indigenous people of South Africa saw a clash of values, particularly when the Europeans sought to impose their capitalist society on the communal societies of the region. From the start, the local people resisted this imposition and the stage was set for three centuries of conflict and oppression.

Z. Pallo Jordan

I am going to begin my story at the intersection of the colonial capitalist order with the indigenous societies in South Africa. I am not going to trace the history from the arrival of Van Riebeeck in any detail, but will choose what I consider to be the seminal moments in that intersection and the consequences these had for the origins of the ANC.

The moments I am choosing are significant in a number of respects, but especially for marking the transformation of South Africa from what had existed at the time Van Riebeeck arrived. We begin with two societies confronting each other across frontiers and proceed to uncover the evolution of a common society in which there is no longer a frontier, but in which the people of South Africa, white and black, live together within one economy.

In the previous section Kgalema Motlanthe, in sketching the evolution of society in general, talked about the differences between the mode of production in South Africa before colonialism and the mode of production imported to South Africa from Europe. These two modes of production could be regarded as two distinct societies in the beginning. On the one hand, there was the colonial society – Dutch, later British, or Anglo-Dutch if you like – and on the other hand, there were the indigenous societies. Indigenous societies were, primarily, communally based societies in which property was collectively owned. In contrast, Dutch and British colonial society was based on mercantile capitalism, which evolved into agrarian capitalism and later into industrial capitalism. The significant moments I have chosen mark the transition from pre-colonial to colonial modes of production.

The year 1867 saw the opening up of the diggings and mines in Kimberley after the discovery of diamonds. The date is important in that before 1867 the two societies we are discussing lived side by side and engaged in exchange and trade. The members of the two societies interacted with each other at a number of levels. Some on one side crossed into the other, but they remained two distinct and discrete societies.

After the opening up of the mines there was a massive demand for labour, which could only be obtained from the indigenous people themselves. As a result, a mass labour force had to be created and the way it was created is what concerns us here. That process began with the discovery of diamonds and, later, gold and the opening up of mines. It unleashed certain historical forces that led to the situation in which we live today.

The demand for a mass labour force brought about the integration of Africans into the Anglo-Dutch colonial society. At the same time, it led also to the disintegration and destruction of the indigenous modes of production, the collectivist or communal mode that we have noted. All these societies depended on land – for grazing cattle, for cultivation, for hunting and gathering. How then did the colonial administration transform these people who lived on land, who required land and whose whole economic system was dependent on land, into a mass labour force? It did so by taking away their land or by compelling them to leave it. One easy way was to take it by force of arms. The other way was by persuasion: the colonial government created an environment in which the indigenous people were compelled to leave their land and be integrated into the Anglo–Dutch colonial society.

After the opening up of the mines, for a period of about thirty years, an unprecedented level of warfare took place in South Africa. There had been wars before this in South Africa, beginning in 1685 between the Dutch settlers and the Khoikhoi in the Cape. Then came the nine wars between 1779 and 1877 on the frontier in the Eastern Cape; and various wars in what became KwaZulu-Natal, the Free State and the Transvaal. But during the period from about 1870 to 1900, the level of conflict and the number of wars that occurred far outstripped what had happened before. In these thirty years, one could say that virtually all the independent, autonomous, freestanding African communities in South Africa were brought to heel by military means. At the end of these thirty years, African independence and autonomy were totally destroyed in war. Then in 1899 began the last big war of that era, the Anglo–Boer War. All these wars were related to a process unfolding in South Africa at the time – the disintegration of the collectivist African indigenous communities accompanied by the emergence of a dominant Anglo-Dutch colonial society based on mining.

Many have written about the Anglo-Boer War and it is still a very emotional issue. Some argue that it was just a war of aggression, of British imperialism imposing itself on the innocent Afrikaner peasant people in South Africa. That is one way of looking at it. Others view it as a war of liberation. Until recently in Afrikaans literature it was referred to as the *Tweede Vryheidsoorlog*, the Second War of Liberation. That is another perspective. There is yet a third way of looking at it. Today some no longer refer to it as the Anglo-Boer War, but rather as the South African War because all communities in South Africa were involved in it. I like to see it as a revolution from outside and from above, because what the Anglo-Boer War entailed was bringing the political order in South Africa into alignment with what had happened as a result of the opening up of the diamond and gold mines.

The discovery of diamonds led to a massive rush of adventurers into the Kimberley area; many of them were small claim holders. But within the first ten years, the small claim owners had been pushed to the margins and big mining companies emerged and came to dominate the industry in South Africa. This happened first in Kimberley by the 1870s. In the 1880s came the opening of the gold mines on the Witwatersrand, which led to the growth of the city of Johannesburg. As in Kimberley, gold mining was soon dominated by large companies, usually linked to big finance houses. These mining companies and finance houses were controlled by capital from Britain and from British descendants in the Cape and in Natal. The Anglo-Boer War, in a way, brought those economic realities to bear on the political arena of South Africa. British imperialism subjected South Africa to its political domination as an expression of the fact that British capital had become the dominant factor in South African life.

Parallel with the unfolding of these new economic forces in South Africa, there were other changes taking place in the politics of South Africa. Even in early societies, like slavery and feudalism, there is always a class of people who are not necessarily directly involved in production – either as owners or as workers – but are sandwiched somewhere in-between these two major classes. South Africa was no different in this respect.

As a result of what happened between 1652 and the 1870s in South Africa, there emerged among the indigenous people themselves a class of landowners, people who had become farmers. These were not the traditional type of farmer, but the modern type, borrowing and adapting techniques they had learned from Europe and other parts of the world, and actively trading on the market. In the old pre-colonial communal society, one produced as a family; if you had a surplus you might trade that with your neighbours, but in the main you were producing not for the market but for your family, for subsistence. The modern farmer is different in that, while he produces for his subsistence, he produces, in the main, a marketable commodity to sell on the open market. The landowning class of Africans was this type of modern farmer. They were also very much part of the Anglo-Dutch-dominated colonial society. They traded and participated actively within the colonial economy, and they related to the political institutions set up by colonial society, seeking to use its political instruments and institutions for their own aims. They began to organise politically. As a result of the emergence of this landowning class of indigenous people, political organisations began to develop among Africans in the 1880s.

The British had granted the Cape what is referred to as 'representative government' in 1853. This allowed British subjects in the colony to elect their own members of Parliament. In terms of the 1853 Constitution, the franchise was open to all British subjects who had reached the age of 21, were male and earned an annual income of £50 or owned property of £25. In other words, there was a franchise which was not racially based but rather based on ownership of property or income. In terms of the Constitution which granted the Cape representative government, the black landowning classes – African and Coloured – also had the franchise, though they constituted a minority among the electorate.

By the end of the century the majority of Africans incorporated in the Cape Colony did not have the franchise. Those who had been incorporated as workers did not have the vote. Africans living in the Transkei, although their land had been annexed to the Cape Colony, were largely excluded from the franchise according to an Act passed by the white Parliament which nullified communal tenure as a basis for property qualification. In the rest of the Cape the property or income-based franchise, usually referred to as a Whig franchise, was nominally non-racial. In practice, of course, because the majority of blacks in the colony did not own property or have a sufficient income to qualify, it was still a highly racialised franchise.

In 1879 the first African political association was founded in the Cape. Formally known as the Native Educational Association (NEA), it used the instruments of colonial society for its members' own purposes. Soon after his arrival in Natal in 1893, Mohandas Gandhi founded the Natal Indian Congress (NIC) for the property-owning class specifically from the Indian community in that colony. In 1902, in the Western Cape, the African People's Organisation (APO) came into being among the Coloured property-owning class.

The significance of these movements is that they began to pose a vision of what South Africa could be like which differed very sharply from what was emerging as a result of the opening up of the diamond and gold mines. Essentially, what the educated black property-owning classes were saying – to themselves, to society and the government – was that they were all citizens of the British Empire. As such, they enjoyed certain rights and privileges, which were the rights and privileges claimed by all subjects of the Queen, irrespective of their race and on equal terms with the whites.

What were these rights? They were the right to participate in the government of the country through electing representatives directly into Parliament (the franchise); the right of access to property, which would give them the capacity, not only to fend for themselves and support their families, but also to grow and expand economically; the right to practise their professions anywhere and in any fashion they liked, along with other citizens; the right to be able to trade wherever they could, like other British citizens. And they spoke of these rights as the rights of British citizens and British subjects.

Today this may strike many of us as odd. We are talking of people who wanted to bring about change, yet they framed their demands in terms of their being 'subjects of the Queen'. But it is not so odd when you compare it with other similar situations. In 1776, for example, there had been a revolution among the English colonists in North America. What George Washington, Thomas Jefferson and other American revolutionaries argued was that their uprising against the government of King George III was not in order to establish something new and different but because it denied them the rights that were their due as British subjects. And when they were refused, they felt entitled to revolt. In South

Africa, at the beginning of the twentieth century, the demands of Africans, Coloureds and Indians, who were subjects of the British Crown, were not all that different from the American colonists. This was the beginning of their political awakening.

If you look at the world as a British subject who demands the rights due to a British subject, the way you approach politics will be that of someone who sees himself as a loyal subject, insisting on rights which he feels are his due, but which he is only going to obtain from and through the government to which he is appealing. How do you speak to this government? Your posture will not be antagonistic or militant but that of a loyal subject petitioning a government which is regarded as essentially legitimate. The government may have a number of faults, it needs to be pushed here or there a bit, but it is basically acceptable.

This has implications in terms of the strategies you are going to employ. It means you are first going to look for people within the colonial establishment who are willing to listen to and are likely to be sympathetic to your viewpoint. You are going to look for allies among the dominant group within the colonial society. Rather than upset them, or annoy or anger them, you must be out-and-out moderate in your demands, a loyal petitioner who believes that for all its limitations and shortcomings the government will see reason. Moreover, you approach the government in this manner because you see yourself as part of this colonial society. You are

British subjects together with them. That is one of the most important features of the politics of all people in South Africa at the time.

So what changed and brought about a change of mindset? It was the revolution from outside and above that I have referred to – the consequences of the Anglo-Boer War – which brought political institutions in South Africa in line with the economic realities created by the mining revolution. What happened was that just after the war ended, a South African Native Affairs Commission was set up in which the former antagonists, the Boer republicans and the British, came together to form a compact. The central features of this compact were an acknowledgement of the past hostilities and of their differences, and a resolution to let Boer and Brit govern South Africa together on the basis of an alliance against the huge black majority on which they would rely as a mass labour force. The effect of the Native Affairs Commission was that it brought about a change in how the black majority was viewed. Before 1905, they were treated in the Cape at least as potential citizens of the Empire with certain rights and as British subjects, albeit second-class citizens and second-class British subjects. After 1905, they ceased being citizens altogether, even second-class citizens, and became just subjects.

What was agreed by the Native Affairs Commission was that all people who were not of direct European descent would no longer have any claims of citizenship

– most of all, a claim to the right to vote and participate directly in government, and then all the related rights. They were henceforth to be regarded as a conquered people; a subject people who had no rights and who would be ruled as such. This brought about an enormous change, not only in the manner in which South Africa would be administered thereafter, but also in the thinking of black political leaders.

In order to understand what happened, let us look at the career of two people who came into prominence at around the same time during the 1880s. The one was John Tengo Jabavu, the first African publisher in this country, founder of the newspaper *Imvo Zabantsundu*, spokesman of African opinion in the Cape and also election agent for the white liberal Cape politician James Rose-Innes.

Jabavu had been associated with the educational institution of Lovedale and its paper, *Isigidimi Sama Xosa*, which he broke with in the 1880s because the newspaper had supported some of the worst atrocities committed by British troops during the 'Gun War' in Lesotho at the time. He then established his own newspaper, *Imvo Zabantsundu*, which means 'Black Opinion'. Jabavu became, in a sense, the spokesperson of the class of educated landowning blacks in the Cape. His approach to politics was: 'Yes, we are good British subjects, we have the right to vote, we even have the right to run for election, but we should not do so because if we do, we are going to upset many of our white friends who, in spite of being our friends, have lots of prejudices and do not trust us. So let us rather elect moderate, liberal whites who will be sympathetic to the cause of the blacks, and maybe they can be the ones who fight our battles in the corridors of power.'

The other black leader of the time was W.B. Rubusana, almost an exact contemporary of Jabavu. Deriving from the same stratum of landowning Africans in the Eastern Cape, he also founded a newspaper, *Izwi Labantu*, with a slightly different approach: 'Yes, we are British subjects, we have these rights. We can be elected, we can elect, but we shouldn't place so much reliance on our "friends"; we should be more reliant on ourselves and, where it is necessary, we should intervene and actually enter the corridors of power ourselves.' This came to pass shortly after Union, when in 1911 Rubusana ran for a seat on the Cape Provincial Council and won. His decision to stand was opposed by Jabavu. This tells us something about how the African elite was beginning to change: starting out with Jabavu and people who said, 'Let's put our faith in liberal white representatives', and ending up with Rubusana, who said, 'That's all well and good, but let us act on our own behalf.'

Much of the history of South Africa after the Native Affairs Commission was taken up with the Convention movement, which finally led to the formation of Union in 1910. This movement had two divergent strands – one black, the other white. The Union of 1910 was, in a sense, the final seal on the pact arrived at through the Native Affairs Commission. As a concession to the Cape's existing non-racial franchise, the former Boer Republics of the Transvaal and Free State conceded to blacks in the Cape their franchise but with this caveat: that while they could vote, they could not be elected to the Union Parliament. The Transvaal and Orange Free State, on the other hand, would retain their racist policies and practices – no blacks could become electors, let alone be elected. The franchise would be exclusively white. This arrangement became the dominant feature of South African politics after 1910. It was in reaction to this that the African National Congress was formed within two years after Union.

In many senses, the ANC was the brainchild of the stratum of landowning Africans who produced the first crop of black professionals. In addition to investing their money in land, they also invested it in education and it was from among them that a growing number of young people were sent from South Africa to study abroad, to the United States and to Britain. It is from among many of these foreign-educated Africans that the idea emerged of forming the African National Congress.

Jabavu, Rubusana and their generation, the founders of the African political tradition in South Africa, virtually all received their training and education in South Africa. The people who founded the ANC, in the main, received their education in the United States and Britain. This marks an important distinction between the two groups. In addition to the generational difference, there was also an experiential difference. Experientially, the foreign-educated (especially American-educated) members of the elite were very conscious of the fact that the position of black South Africans was a universal condition of people of African descent. They had been to the United States and Britain, where they had rubbed shoulders with Africans from other parts of the world, and realised that nowhere did Africans govern themselves. All Africans were colonial subjects, with the exception of two countries, Ethiopia and Liberia; everywhere else Africans and people of African descent were governed by others. There was a potent consciousness of this situation among the new crop of young African leaders who were educated overseas. This is what was later referred to as a 'pan-Africanist' vision, which was pronounced very eloquently by Pixley kaIsaka Seme, in a speech at Columbia University in 1906, when he spoke about the future of Africa, the possibilities of Africa, the rebirth of Africa.

The second important distinction between the two groups concerns also the fields of endeavour in which they were involved. The first crop of African professionals – like Jabavu, Rubusana and their contemporaries – consisted of landowners, teachers or ministers of religion. Rubusana himself was a Congregational minister. In the new generation, though one did find some men of the cloth, in the main they were young professionals. The three most prominent – Seme, Alfred Mangena and Richard Msimang – were all lawyers. In addition to their pan-African vision, they were also independent professionals and self-employed.

Thirdly, the new generation also had experience of the so-called mother country, the colonising power itself, Britain, and its political institutions. They were much more familiar with it, at first hand, than the previous generation. It was this new generation who would recognise the need for a national organisation.

During the period of the Convention movement leading up to Union, a number of African deputations visited London, to persuade the British government not to allow the passage of the Act of Union because of its racist franchise clauses. When the last such deputation arrived in 1909, the members met a young man who had just finished his Bar exam in London, Pixley kaIsaka Seme, who planted the notion of an African National Congress.

The Act of Union came about on 31 May 1910. In October 1911, Pixley Seme wrote a letter, published in Jabavu's *Imvo Zabantsundu*, calling for the convening of a 'Native National Congress' because he believed that the tribal differences, animosities and disunity among the Africans were the cause of their troubles. If they were to uproot the demon of racism from the country, they had to leave behind them the disunity of the African people. They were one people and must act as one people. This was a very important step forward because it indicated the emergence of a national consciousness, no longer rooted in the pre-colonial past.

SELF-DETERMINATION

Z. Pallo Jordan & Jeff Radebe

Z. Pallo Jordan

In the past we used to characterise the political and economic system in South Africa before 1994 as 'colonialism of a special type'. Though this is a formulation that has been challenged by many people, I think it is essentially correct. Earlier, I referred to the fact that the educated landowning class of black people who emerged at the end of the nineteenth century regarded themselves as citizens of the British Empire, people who had rights and who claimed those rights. The 1905 Native Affairs Commission put an end to that by declaring black people throughout South Africa as subject people, who would henceforth be ruled as colonial subjects. To underline that reality, well into the 1960s the department of government charged with the responsibility of administering the oppressive laws that governed the lives of Africans was referred to as the 'Native Affairs Department' – not Home Affairs but 'Native Affairs', which made it clear that the people who governed the country did not see themselves as natives of the country. The natives were those people who were being governed, while the rulers saw themselves as foreigners who were governing natives. That is the most eloquent expression of the colonial relationship between those who governed and the indigenous people.

If one looks at the laws that ruled the lives of natives, they were like those of an occupying army in a foreign country. The movement of natives was controlled by passes and other forms of control to make sure that the state knew exactly where they were at any time. This is what an occupying foreign army does, not an indigenous government. So, the term we used to employ to describe the South African polity, 'colonialism of a special type', had a great deal of relevance and was very close to the reality. What we did not necessarily analyse, as we should have, was what that 'colonialism of a special type' consisted of.

Firstly, political power was explicitly a monopoly of the whites; they had the vote and controlled state institutions. Secondly, whites monopolised the economic power as well, as can be seen in the 1913 Natives Land Act, which set aside 13 per cent of the land area of South Africa for the natives, and 87 per cent for whites. It would be difficult to find a more eloquent expression of the monopolisation of economic power. Thirdly, the system occurring in South Africa was basically one of labour coercion, in which a number of institutions and laws were used to compel the indigenous people, the 'natives', to make themselves available as cheap labour power. Fourthly, because the system was so evidently unfair, it had to be authoritarian, so there were a myriad of laws to back up the system of colonialism of a special type, which deprived black South Africans of rights that people take for granted in other parts of the world.

So, when we talk about self-determination in South Africa, it meant overthrowing the system of colonialism of a special type. In the first instance, what overthrowing the system of colonialism meant was the attempt to deracialise the franchise and break the political monopoly of the minority over the country's institutions. Secondly, it meant addressing the issue of the monopoly of economic power; thirdly, dismantling the system of labour coercion; and fourthly, abolishing the authoritarian system of government.

In 1964 Nelson Mandela prepared a speech for the Rivonia Trial, entitled 'Why I Am Prepared to Die'. It sets out in very clear terms how he understood the right of self-determination. I want to draw your attention to the latter part of the quotation: 'The Magna Carta, the Petition of Rights, and the Bill of Rights are documents which are held in veneration by democrats throughout the world. I have a great respect for British political institutions and for the country's system of justice. I regard the British Parliament as the most democratic institution in the world and the independence and impartiality of this judiciary, never fail to arouse my admiration. The American Congress, that country's doctrine of separation of powers, as well as the independence of this judiciary, arouse in me similar sentiments. I have been influenced in my thinking by both West and East. All this has led me to feel that in my search for a political formula, I should be absolutely impartial and objective. I should tie myself to no particular system of society other than of socialism. I must leave myself free to borrow the best from the West and from the East.'

Though we may have differences of opinion among ourselves about whether the British Parliament is the most democratic in the world, Mandela's speech sets out certain ideals and principles to which the ANC has subscribed from the very beginning. These include the notion of rights, of inherent human rights, embodied in and evolving from the Magna Carta, through to latter-day declarations of human rights and our own national Constitution. This is the one value to which the ANC has subscribed from the very beginning, and which is central to the notion of national self-determination as understood by the ANC.

The second principle is of democratic institutions, including an independent judiciary: this is another value to which the ANC has subscribed and which is central to its notion of self-determination. When Mandela spoke at Rivonia about borrowing the best from the East and the West and about binding himself to the system of socialism, he was suggesting that the economic system which the ANC wanted to see in South Africa was socialism. Others have imputed something else, but

I think the idea is of an economic system that is not coercive and that will benefit the majority of the people of our country.

But, most importantly, the ideas and values embodied in the speech by Mandela link the ANC to a particular political tradition – a political tradition which derives from the great revolutions of the eighteenth century and which evolved in the twentieth century as a human rights culture culminating in the Universal Declaration of Human Rights. The ANC has always been located very firmly within this particular tradition of human rights and has seen itself as part of the tradition. It is what we have always understood as national self-determination.

When the ANC was founded in 1912, the founding members would have felt comfortable with many of these things that Mandela said at Rivonia, though they would have added that they didn't think the majority of our people were ready to exercise these rights. When the ANC adopted its first programmatic statement in 1925, it was called the 'African Bill of Rights'. This statement spoke in terms of 'the vote for all civilised men' – not women, not people, but 'civilised men'! By this they meant the definition derived from the Cape Colony's Constitution of 1853 – people who owned property, who earned an income of a certain value, who had a certain level of education.

It took another twenty years for the ANC to outgrow this notion, when it adopted the 'Africans' Claims' document in 1943. The 'Africans' Claims', in contrast to the 'African Bill of Rights', does not speak in terms of 'equal rights for civilised men'. It speaks of government by the consent of the governed – a very different notion because it speaks of the people who are governed as the ones who ought to decide who should govern them. This is the notion of self-determination as commonly understood. From 'rights for all civilised men' to the 'right to government by the consent of the governed' was a step of great importance in the history of the ANC.

Jeff Radebe

Following on from the discussion by Pallo Jordan, my brief is to try to reinforce what he has covered, focusing on the historical roots of ANC policy. We need to ask questions about the emphasis at the time of the formation of the ANC in 1912, what drove the policy positions of the time and what has changed in ANC policy since then. I will draw largely on the views expressed by Pixley kaIsaka Seme, an early ANC leader, as well as others who contributed to the formation of the ANC.

One of the primary reasons for the formation of the ANC in 1912 was the subjugation of our people, who had been forced to become wage labourers in the new economy opened up by the development of mining. Another was the exclusion of Africans from any share in the political system in the Union of South Africa and the closure of all reasonable avenues of engagement by African leaders with the white colonial and British authorities. The delegation of African leaders dispatched to Britain to argue for the accommodation of Africans in the Union of South Africa was rebuffed and their requests and petitions were rejected by the colonial masters. We can see that the conditions that prevailed in South Africa at this time dictated the kind of tactics our leaders pursued then. We can contrast this with the decision by the ANC in 1960 to adopt the armed struggle against the apartheid regime and in 1990 to suspend armed action as a result of the Groote Schuur

Minute. This returned the ANC to its original approach of seeking a negotiated settlement in South Africa.

ꙨꙨꙨ

We need to recall the link between the founding leaders of the ANC and the institution of traditional leadership. When the ANC was established, a critical role was played by various kings and traditional leaders, not only from South Africa but from the whole of southern Africa, some of whom sent representatives to the 1912 meeting because their status prevented them from attending meetings with 'commoners'. Among them were Letsie of Basutoland, Gaseitsiwe of the Bangwaketse and Lekoko of the Baralong, both in the Bechuanaland Protectorate. These and other traditional leaders wanted to use the platform that was being created in the Congress to regain the power they had lost due to colonial wars. In terms of the constitution adopted at the founding congress, twenty-two traditional leaders, including the deposed Zulu king Dinuzulu, were accorded the status of honorary presidents. They formed the Upper House of the Congress, whose role was to advise and guide the 'executive commoners'. It is important to remember this because we still face the challenge of how to deal with the institutions of traditional leadership. We are still trying to find out, as the ANC, how to include traditional authority in government in all relevant areas and what the role and function is of traditional leadership for the future.

The formation of the ANC resulted in Congress becoming the real Parliament of the South African people. Even today, we remain of the view that the ANC is the real Parliament of the people. Its task is to build democratic institutions that represent the people of South Africa. The vision that Seme announced in his address at Columbia University in 1906 – 'The African people … possess a common fundamental sentiment' – is as relevant today as it was then. Today, in fact, we have an even broader vision as the ANC – embracing non-racialism and non-sexism – which derives from the 1985 Kabwe Conference, where it was decided that all racial groups in South Africa, not only Africans, could be members of the ANC and could be represented in its leadership structures.

Because the formation of the ANC had been preceded by colonial wars and the defeat of Africans, the issue of unity was of paramount importance in 1912 – bringing together all the tribal groupings to form one South African nation. When the ANC was formed, people came from all around southern Africa wearing different attire, emphasising their different tribal origins. But at the founding congress there was a call for unity in spite of all the differences that existed. The song or hymn that was sung at the opening congress of the ANC in 1912 was 'Nkosi Sikelel' iAfrika' ('God Bless Africa') by Enoch Sontonga. Today, almost a hundred years later, we still feel strongly that unity in the ANC and in South Africa as a whole is the golden thread that keeps the

ANC together. We are one nation though with many cultures and our Constitution acknowledges our unity in diversity.

In 1912, the leadership of the ANC emphasised education because most of them were very well-educated, some having attended university abroad, in particular the United States and Britain. They used the knowledge they acquired there for the benefit of South Africa. There is a very beautiful quote by Seme in his Columbia University speech on how educated people need to return to their country of birth. He said: 'The ancestral greatness, the unimpaired genius, and the recuperative power of the race, its irrepressibility, which assures its permanence, constitute the African's greatest source of inspiration. He has refused to camp forever on the borders of the industrial world; having learned that knowledge is power, he is educating his children. You find them in Edinburgh, in Cambridge, and in the great schools of Germany. These return to their country like arrows, to drive darkness from the land.' Leaders like Seme were at the forefront of the establishment of the ANC and chose to lead our people to freedom instead of concentrating on their own personal interests, even though they aimed at assimilation into the social and political system of the time. When we look at the ANC today, our manifesto still emphasises the importance of education.

Seme's educational and other initiatives can be regarded as positive evidence of his untiring devotion to the process of regeneration in Africa. Today his message is still being reinforced by the ANC, as it tackles the issues of improving our continent and the world. We are committed to making Africa and the world a better place for all. At the time of its foundation the ANC sought to respond to the social and economic conditions of black South Africans. In his speech of 1906 Seme spoke about Africans' refusal to camp forever on the borders of the industrial world. His words need to inspire us to fulfil their vision today. For the effects of landlessness, land dispossession and rapid urbanisation and industrialisation, which were being felt in his lifetime, still haunt us today. We need to reinforce our efforts to improve our economy, boost employment creation and promote sustainable livelihoods.

ⵔⵔⵔ

While, as I have shown, there are substantial continuities between then and now, some major differences exist between the ANC of 1912 and that of today. Firstly, in 1912 women could not be members of the ANC; patriarchy was clearly a feature of the ANC at the time. Women were only accepted as full members of the ANC in 1943. Today they are fully integrated and play an equal role in the organisation. At the Polokwane conference in 2007 it was resolved that the ANC needs to attain gender parity in all its structures.

Secondly, the ANC of 1912 consisted of gentlemen who believed in petitions, deputations and representations to the powers-that-be; their aim was to be accepted into the political set-up of their colonial masters. This form of political engagement persisted for almost four decades until the 1940s when the ANC Youth League sought to infuse the organisation with a radical programme. In 1949 the ANC adopted the Programme of Action and in the 1950s embarked on the Defiance Campaign and then, in 1960, armed struggle. Tactics are determined by the conditions that exist at any time and need to be adapted accordingly.

Thirdly, the ANC leaders of 1912 were drawn from a small elite of educated, professional Africans. Today the ANC's leadership is drawn from various classes, comprising all ideological persuasions, and driven by the desire to make a better life for all the people of South Africa.

Looking back over almost a century since the ANC was formed, it may seem as if there are many differences, but in terms of policy there have actually been striking continuities. The end of ethnic divisions has always been the driving force behind the striving for unity in the ANC and among all South Africa's people. From the beginning, the issues of land and agriculture were central, but as a result of land dispossession and rapid industrialisation, the issue of worker struggles has become a critical feature of our time. Culture, education and religion have always formed part of a comprehensive approach to addressing the plight of all South Africans. A culture of debate and tolerance of divergences of opinion has existed throughout the history of the ANC, as has an emphasis on international engagement and internationalism in the struggle for a better world. That the tactics and methods of engagement have changed over time has been due to the changing circumstances in which the ANC found itself, circumstances often determined by the brutality of the system it was fighting. Despite these shifts, the issue of unity, which was the foundation stone upon which the ANC was built in 1912, remains central today.

DIVERSE MOVEMENTS
Z. Pallo Jordan & S'bu Ndebele

Z. Pallo Jordan

I want to start with the proposition that the ideology of the ANC is what has over time become the mainstream of African nationalism. What has contributed to this ideology and how has it grown? There are two things to point out about the ANC. The first is its long history among national liberation movements in the world. It was a pioneer movement in sub-Saharan Africa from which a whole host of sister movements drew inspiration. In its early years the ANC drew in people from the so-called British protectorates and beyond, from what was then called Rhodesia (now Zimbabwe), Northern Rhodesia (Zambia) and as far afield as Tanganyika (Tanzania). It influenced them, and when they founded their own local political organisations they called them the African National Congress without exception.

Secondly, we need to look at who the people were that constituted, inspired and formed the ANC. As we have seen, they were a modern, Westernised elite drawn from among the black population. But towards the end of the decade when the ANC was formed, there emerged another important movement – a movement of black workers, in the main African workers, but also Coloured workers, known as the Industrial and Commercial Workers' Union of Africa (ICU). The ICU began as a general workers' union in the Western Cape, but during the 1920s it grew into a mass movement, which spread nationwide, spilling over into the neighbouring territories, in similar fashion to the ANC.

During the early twentieth century, two streams emerged in the national liberation movement. One was led in the main by a modernising, educated elite; and the other came out of the working class. Of course, given the fact that at any time in the history of modern South Africa, the majority of black people, specifically African people, have been workers, these two strands were intertwined. While there always was an elite and, I suppose, there always will be, the majority have been working people. And although the ANC was led and inspired by a modernising elite, it attracted in the main working-class people. The ICU, on the other hand, was organised and set up as a working-class movement. Of course, it also attracted people who were educated and people associated with the elite, but the ANC and the ICU were two independent streams in the beginning. They intersected and interacted as they moved along, and it is that intersection and interaction which shall examine.

One of the distinctive features of African

nationalism as it evolved in South Africa has always been its inclusiveness, its non-racism. There are many reasons why it evolved in that particular manner – some subjective, others objective. The subjective reasons are the values and political ideas that the ANC and the ICU espoused. These are the ideals of democracy, non-racialism and a single nationhood – the view that South Africa, no matter that its population is made up of different racial, linguistic, religious or other elements, is one nation or should be one nation. These were the subjective views of the people who led these movements.

But there are also objective reasons. The borders of South Africa were not determined by the indigenous people of South Africa themselves. As a result people were thrown together from different and unrelated communities into one melting pot. They included people from Europe, people who were the result of sexual unions between Europeans and Africans, people who came from the East, from the Indian Ocean islands and other parts of Africa, and the indigenous people of South Africa themselves, who came from diverse linguistic and ethnic backgrounds. All were brought together into a single society, however deeply divided it was. This was the objective reality that existed at the beginning of the twentieth century and the ANC was forced to face up to it. Even if it had thought or felt differently, it would have been compelled to be inclusive. In the 1950s, for example, the Pan Africanist Congress broke away from the ANC and started out as a congress purely of Africans. But two years into its existence, in the Western Cape the PAC had Coloured leaders. By the time its leaders went into exile and set up offices in places like Algeria, the PAC even had a white representative. So, the objective reality of a South Africa made up of many different elements and people imposed itself on the PAC, despite what the PAC leadership thought and wanted. They had to face up to the reality. Thus when we talk about the reasons why the nationalism that evolved in South Africa was inclusive, there are both subjective and objective reasons.

Before the 1870s South Africa consisted of two societies confronting each other across frontiers: a discrete African society on one side and a distinct colonial society on the other. But after the mining revolution, the boundaries began to disappear and a common society began to emerge. That too is an objective reality. When the white minority oppressor group faced up to the objective reality that black and white lived together in South Africa, they sought to structure the relationship between black and white so that it would always remain essentially a colonial one in which the blacks were dominated by the whites. In contrast, the response of the national liberation movement was to try to overturn the colonial relationship and create a society of equals. Hence their insistence on non–racism.

How could one achieve a South Africa which belongs to all who live in it, to quote the Freedom Charter?

One could only do so by dismantling the colonial relationship between black and white and establishing a democracy. Thus democracy and liberation became inseparable, and likewise democracy and non-racialism. The objective reality of South Africa's multi-lingual, multi-racial, multi-ethnic, multi-faith society can only be realised through democracy. These were the values that the national liberation movement came to espouse.

The national liberation movement also grew out of diverse backgrounds. On the one hand there was the ANC, inspired and led in the main by a modernising black elite. What was different about the elite who led the ANC was that its members came from diverse backgrounds but shared certain things in common. They began to see themselves as distinct and different from the rest of the African society. Usually, they were Christians. With Christianity came literacy; members of the elite had usually been to school – in those days they were referred to as 'School people'. In contrast, the majority of the African population were not necessarily Christian and had not attended school – in those days they were usually referred to as the 'Red people', because of the red blankets that many used to wear. The other distinct feature of the elite was that in the main they were property-owners; or else they had a certain level of skill and a certain level of income.

Because they saw themselves as distinct, as school-educated, literate Christians and small property-owners, they led lives rather different from the rest of

African society. They were not bound by the former parameters of ethnic group, language and geography that others still recognised. Given the demographic geography of South Africa at the time, if for example you came from the Eastern Cape you were very likely to be Xhosa-speaking and to marry someone who was Xhosa-speaking. But members of the African elite met, interacted with and related to people from other language and ethnic groups in the mission schools, education institutions and churches which they attended, and did not share the same sort of cultures any longer. Thus someone who came from the Eastern Cape might marry someone from the Northern Cape, and someone in the Northern Cape might marry someone from the Transvaal. All these factors make for a different type of consciousness. A Xhosa-speaker who marries someone who is Tswana-speaking and a Venda-speaker who marries someone who is Zulu-speaking do not think of themselves and their children as Xhosa or Venda, Zulu or Tswana anymore. For individuals this meant the emergence of a new identity, as an African sharing a common position in the society, and common grievances, with other Africans. As a result of this intermixing and interaction between people from diverse backgrounds, we see therefore the emergence of a new consciousness, what one might call a national consciousness, which was rooted in certain material realities.

The same thing happened with the working class

as well. Men recruited to work in the mines would come across fellow miners from all over southern Africa; they would be spoken to in Fanagalo by the bosses, treated alike and forced to carry passes. Being thrown together like this created an objective situation in which people were brought together by material factors beyond their control. They had to relate to people from other ethnic groups because they worked with them and lived together. And when they wanted higher wages, they needed to act together. They could no longer hold to their various old identities. They just had to be workers, specifically African workers, because they all carried passes. So there again, on the mines, in the docks, on the railways, the objective situation created conditions for the emergence of a national consciousness.

Into this mixed bag came, as a result of industrialisation, an immigrant group in the main drawn from Europe. These were workers who arrived in South Africa during the rush for gold and diamonds, and they brought with them, in their baggage, traditions of working-class organisation, including ideas of socialism and humanism. As early as the 1870s there arose among the white diggers in Kimberley the demand that no one who was not white be allowed to prospect for or deal in diamonds. Other demands were that anyone who was not white had to carry a permit from a magistrate, and when they ceased to work on the mines, they had to leave the area. This was not

Ray Alexander with members of the Food & Canning Workers' Union

Bill Andrews

Yusuf Cachalia

Yusuf Dadoo

John Dube

Ruth First

Bram Fischer

Michael Harmel

Helen Joseph

Moses Kotane

Alex La Guma

Albert Luthuli

Moses Mabhida

Nelson Mandela

J.B. Marks

Ida Mtwana

Lilian Ngoyi

Z.K. Matthews

Duma Nokwe

Reg September

Walter Sisulu

Oliver Tambo

Congress of the People, Kliptown, 1955

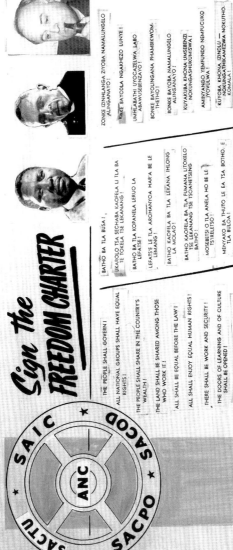

Sign the FREEDOM CHARTER

(SAIC · SACOD · ANC · SACTU · SACPO)

THE PEOPLE SHALL GOVERN!

ALL NATIONAL GROUPS SHALL HAVE EQUAL RIGHTS!

THE PEOPLE SHALL SHARE IN THE COUNTRY'S WEALTH!

THE LAND SHALL BE SHARED AMONG THOSE WHO WORK IT!

ALL SHALL BE EQUAL BEFORE THE LAW!

ALL SHALL ENJOY EQUAL HUMAN RIGHTS!

THERE SHALL BE WORK AND SECURITY!

THE DOORS OF LEARNING AND OF CULTURE SHALL BE OPENED!

THERE SHALL BE HOUSES, SECURITY AND COMFORT!

THERE SHALL BE PEACE AND FRIENDSHIP!

BATHO BA TLA BUSA!,

LIKAROLO TSA SECHABA KAOFELA LI TLA BA TE TOKELA TSE LEKANANG!

BATHO BA TLA KOPANELA LERUO LA LEFATSE!

LEFATSE LE TLA AROHANYOA HARA BE LE LEMANG!

BATHO KAOFELA BA TLA LEKANA IHLONG LA MOLAO!

BATHO KAOFELA BA TLA FUMANA LITOKELO TSE LEKANANG TSE TSOANETSENG BATHO!

MOSEBETSI O TLA ANELA HO BE LE TSIRELETSO!

MENYAKO EA THUTO LE EA TSA BOTHO, E TLA BULOA!

HO TLA BA MATLO, TSIRELETSO, LE HO LULA MOTHO A PHOTHOLLOHILE!

HO TLA BA KHOTSO LE SELEKANE!!

ZONKE IZINHLANGA ZIYOBA NAMALUNGELO ALINGANAYO!

ONKE BAYODLA NGAKHEZO LUNYE!

UMHLABATHI UYOCAZELWA LABO ABAWUSEBENZAYO!

BONKE BAYOLUNGANA PHAMBIKWOM-THETHO!

BONKE BAYOBA NAMALUNGELO ALINGANAYO!

KUYAKUBA KHONA UMSEBENZI NOKUNGASHUKUMISWA!

AMINYANGO YEMFUNDO NEMPUCUKO IYOVULWA!

KUYOBA KHONA IZINDLU NOKUNGATHIKAMEZWA NOKUTHO-KOMALA!

KUYAKUBAKHONA UXOLO NOBUDLELWANE!

something that came from the government, but from the white diggers in Kimberley, and the government was forced to respond to their demands. Here lie the beginnings of the racially exclusive monopoly of the modern economy that characterised South Africa for more than a century. If you couldn't own a mine or deal in or dig for diamonds, it meant you could only be on the mines if you worked. And as a worker on the diamond fields, your movements were controlled by the permit from the magistrate which allowed you to stay only as long as you remained a worker.

Further steps were taken down the road to white dominance. When the mining companies began to lose money as a result of theft by workers who hid diamonds on their bodies, they set up a whole system of controls, including the establishment of compounds where the workers were forced to live. In this way a compound labour system began on the diamond fields in order to control the workers. As a result a working class, predominantly black, emerged on the diamond fields, which suffered distinct disadvantages. In the beginning, the mine bosses tried to search everyone who came out of the mines, but the white workers went on strike and defended themselves at the expense of the black workers. Here is the beginning of a white working class, which saw itself as distinct and apart from the indigenous working class – in fact as part of the privileged white colonial society as against the 'natives'. In this way the socialist ideas that came in the baggage of white workers from Europe were tainted by racist practices in South Africa.

What brought matters to a head was that, with the development of the mining industry, larger and larger numbers of African workers were drawn in, and at a certain point they came to outnumber the whites, though they were still confined mainly to unskilled labour. During the early twentieth century, the mine owners thought that one of the ways they could solve their problems was by reducing their costs. As any good unionist will tell you, the fastest way a boss can reduce his costs is by getting cheaper labour and paying lower wages. So the mine owners decided to end the reservation of skilled work for white workers and open it up to the blacks while paying them lower wages than the whites.

One of the responses of white workers was to resist. The other response was to embrace the black workers and draw them into the labour movement. Those who championed the latter course were usually from the left wing of the white labour movement. Things came to a head after the First World War, when the white workers on the Rand went out on a general strike in 1922 to defend their exclusive right to skilled work. It took the form of bloody confrontations, with pitched battles in the streets of Johannesburg and aerial bombing of certain white working-class suburbs by the air force until the strike was suppressed. At the end of the day, even though the white workers were defeated, the outcome did not actually open up skilled work for the black workers. As a result of that experience, the left wing of the white labour movement turned from an emphasis on the organisation of white workers to the organisation of black workers. In a similar way the national liberation movement, both in its elite (the ANC) and in its working-class components (the ICU), had embraced the idea of a common and single nationhood – of South Africa belonging to all who live in it, black and white.

The left wing of the white labour movement broke with the right wing at the outbreak of the First World War in 1914, and constituted itself as the International Socialist League (ISL). When the Russian Revolution took place in 1917, the ISL was amongst the first to support the October Revolution. When the Bolsheviks set up the Communist International in 1919, the ISL sought affiliation with it. After the 1922 Rand strike, there was a complete split between the left and right wings in the white labour movement. The right wing did not support the Russian Revolution, did not identify with the black working class in South Africa, and did not support a single nationhood. This became one of the crucial distinctions between left and right in the labour movement in South Africa.

During the 1920s, the ICU grew at a rapid pace. Through the ICU, a number of important working-class militants received their first political training and in due course came to play a large role in the ANC and in its evolution. Among them were A.W.G. Champion from Natal, Gana Makabeni, Johnny Gomas and James La Guma (father of Alex La Guma), the last two both Coloured workers from the Western Cape. Because of the interaction and intersection with the ANC at various levels, these ICU officials became important players in the ANC and began to influence the ANC's thinking and politics.

The growth of the ICU in the 1920s so impressed some of the ANC leaders, especially Josiah Gumede, who became its president in 1927, that they began to rethink the way the ANC leadership looked at the world and at itself. Whereas previously the ANC had relied in the main on petitions and deputations, believing that they could expect reasonableness on the other side of the table, Gumede began to realise that they had leverage, the means to force those in power to give them what they wanted provided they use the organised strength of their people. So the ANC came to see the need to develop the organisation as a movement of ordinary working people – people working on the land, farm workers, industrial workers, mineworkers – led by the elite. Gumede's rethinking of the role of the ANC coincided with the tenth anniversary of the Russian Revolution. In 1927, inspired by the Communist International, a congress was held in Brussels by a group called the League Against Imperialism, to which Gumede was invited together with James La Guma. Returning from Brussels, Gumede addressed the ANC conference and spoke about the leverage that the black majority could exert to win their rights.

In November 1927 both Gumede and La Guma were invited to attend the tenth anniversary celebrations of the Revolution in Moscow; from there the two men travelled to many of the Asiatic Soviet republics and were impressed with what the communists had done in these underdeveloped countries – Third World countries if you like – that had been part of the Tsarist Empire. Gumede came back and spoke of having seen the 'New Jerusalem'; he now knew the way forward.

It is from the mingling of all these ideas and processes – the emergence of the ANC and ICU in the 1910s, the growth of the ICU during the 1920s, the impact of the Russian Revolution, the influence of the ISL, which evolved into the Communist Party of South Africa – that a vision of a new South Africa developed within the ANC. In due course this vision crystallised in the Freedom Charter, which is still the programme of the ANC today.

S'bu Ndebele

The period of the ANC's history that I will deal with here is the 1920s and 1930s, when it faced many of the questions that confront us still today. On the face of things, these were lean years for the organisation. Unlike the Tripartite Alliance of today, the ANC, the Communist Party and the workers' movement in the 1920s were mostly separate and competing bodies, though a number of individuals were members of more than one body. Like the 'broad church' ANC of today, the ANC of the 1920s and 1930s combined both moderates and radicals within its membership and leadership, though for most of the time it was led by the sort of educated, professional elite who had founded the organisation in 1912.

In its ability to mobilise black people the ANC proved less successful than the other major movement of the time, the Industrial and Commercial Workers' Union, which stood at the forefront of black opposition in the 1920s. In the late 1920s the first African trade unions began to be formed and there was a growth in worker action. The Communist Party, founded in 1921, also began to compete for black membership, particularly after it adopted the thesis of the Native Republic. In 1929 the party adopted a strategic line which held that 'The most direct line of advance to socialism runs through the mass struggle for majority rule'. Here for the first time, the relation between the 'national revolution' and the 'socialist revolution' was enunciated in the South African context.

Many of the leading figures in the ANC of the time were troubled by the radical turn that was being taken in black politics. However, one group in the ANC, centred on Josiah Gumede, who became president of the ANC in 1927, showed leanings towards the Communist Party. Communist influence was also strong in the Western Cape branch of the ANC, where Elliot Tonjeni and Bransby Ndobe sought to cooperate with local communists. Gumede also took a leading part in the League of African Rights, formed in 1929, along with white communists like Sidney Bunting and Eddie Roux. The League, which bridged the Communist Party and the more radical wing of the ANC, never gained much prominence and soon disappeared from the scene.

Within the ANC the divisions between moderates and radicals came to a head in 1930 when Gumede was replaced as president by the more traditional figure of Pixley Seme. Devoid of the energising ideas of the Communist Party and lacking the mass base of the workers' movement, the ANC over the following few years began to fade away.

It was the passage of Prime Minister J.B.M. Hertzog's 'Native' Acts of 1936 that brought about the revival of African resistance in the country. One of these, the Native Trust and Land Act, added to and strengthened the measures introduced by the infamous 1913 Land Act to control African tenants on white farms and to limit the amount of land set aside for exclusive African occupation. Another, the Representation of

Natives Act, withdrew from Africans in the Cape the longstanding right to vote based on a property and income qualification. In lieu of representation in Parliament it set in place a Natives' Representative Council, on which twelve indirectly elected Africans would sit with four African nominees and white native commissioners. This NRC would be purely advisory in its function – 'a toy telephone' as it was later derisively called.

The announcement of these segregation measures galvanised black opposition. In late 1935 a new body, the All-African Convention, came into being after an inaugural meeting was held in Bloemfontein that was attended by over four hundred delegates, many of them ANC figures. Within the AAC the assembly of a broad spread of organisations representing black people throughout South Africa was truly impressive – it was probably the largest single protest in black politics till then – but once the Hertzog Bills were passed into law, the AAC went into decline. Though there were later debates about the need to maintain a united front of black organisations, the ANC continued to regard itself as the sole mouthpiece of the African people. And while the AAC faded away, the ANC was reinvigorated in the 1940s by its Youth League and entered on a new phase of its history.

THE CONGRESS ALLIANCE

Nkosazana Dlamini-Zuma & Ben Turok

Nkosazana Dlamini-Zuma

From its inception, the ANC's character has remained more or less the same, though the terrain and means of struggle have changed – from petitions to mass struggles and armed struggle. Today the ANC is the ruling party in a new democracy and basically represents the overwhelming majority of the people. From the first the ANC stood for the liberation of the black people in general, and Africans in particular, not only because the Africans were the majority, but also because they were those most oppressed and exploited. The content of the struggle had to reflect this reality. But though the ANC had to ensure mass mobilisation of the African people, clearly the Africans were not the only oppressed national group. Indian and Coloured people also suffered varying forms of oppression, humiliation and discrimination. Unity in action with all oppressed people was fundamental to the liberation struggle. Historically, Indian and Coloured

65

people have participated at every level of the struggle – and mobilisation of these communities formed part of the intensification of the struggle throughout the ANC's history.

Indian immigrants first arrived in South Africa in 1860 as indentured labourers to work on the sugarcane plantations of Natal. Their living conditions were very bad and they earned a pittance. When released from their indentured status, they found employment as mineworkers, general labourers, council workers and market gardeners. But even as free men, they did not escape humiliation and insults to their dignity. They were segregated into designated residential areas and were even prohibited from living in the Orange Free State or passing through it without a permit. In 1893 a young British-trained lawyer named Mohandas Gandhi arrived in Natal to fight a legal case for an Indian merchant. After his arrival, he was confronted with the reality of South Africa. He himself was thrown off a train for occupying a first-class compartment, then considered the preserve of whites, even though he had a valid ticket. He ended up becoming active in the struggles of the Indian people in South Africa and played a large role in the establishment of the Natal Indian Congress and its mouthpiece, the journal *Indian Opinion*.

After the Second World War, and at much the same time that the Youth League was reinvigorating and radicalising the ANC, the Natal Indian Congress and the Transvaal Indian Congress were taken over by a new generation of activists who had nothing but contempt for the old-style politics of deference. Dr G.M. Naicker became president of the Natal Congress and Dr Yusuf Dadoo president of the Transvaal Congress. Under their leadership these organisations became committed to unity in action with the ANC and other progressive black bodies. The Xuma–Naicker–Dadoo Pact of 1947 foreshadowed both the Defiance Campaign of 1952, in which the ANC and the South African Indian Congress undertook a joint campaign of defiance against unjust laws, and the Congress of the People in 1955.

Until the 1940s, the Indian congresses were not really mass-based organisations. It was the passage of the Asiatic Land Tenure and Indian Representation Act in 1946 (the so-called Ghetto Act), which aimed to confine Indians to specific areas and prevent their 'penetration' of white areas, that saw the launch of a popular campaign of passive resistance led by Dr Naicker. At one point two thousand people who participated in this campaign were arrested and imprisoned, including three hundred women. Africans, Coloureds and whites also joined in and some of them were arrested and imprisoned. The slogans and speeches of the time give a sense of the public sentiment: 'Down with the Ghetto Bills, to hell with the Ghetto Bills.'

I want to quote a few messages of support for this campaign to illustrate my point. One came from an African comrade: 'The present struggle is not a struggle of the Indian people alone. It is part of the struggle of the oppressed people of the world. By struggle, we also can liberate our people. I am prepared to go back to prison, for we must make the necessary sacrifices. I appeal to all the non-European people to join in a mighty battle for freedom.'

This resistance was seen as a general mass mobilisation not only by and for the Indians. The ANC Youth League at the time sent this message of unity in action: 'We salute the Indian people who resolve to carry on the struggle against the colour bar and race domination as a struggle for fundamental human rights.' So there was a coalition of forces in support of the resistance campaign in the late 1940s.

The Coloured community has its own very rich history of struggle. The history of independent Coloured political activity goes back to the late 1800s, at a time when Coloured people in the Cape were supposed to enjoy equal political rights with whites on the basis of a colour-blind qualified franchise. However, it became clear that even these limited and circumscribed rights were increasingly under threat and in 1902 the African People's Organisation was formed by a group of Coloured leaders in Cape Town. This soon spread to other towns in the country. It is interesting that the first Coloured organisation was called the African People's Organisation and not the Coloured People's Organisation. In a way, it was a pioneer for the Congress Movement as the first black political organisation functioning at a national level. Sol Plaatje, who was involved in the founding of the ANC, belonged to a branch of the APO in Kimberley. During much of the first half of the twentieth century the leader of the APO was Dr Abdullah Abdurahman.

The APO responded to the British government's approval of the Act of Union, which did not extend the franchise in the new South Africa to black people as a whole, in this way: 'The struggle has not ended, it has just begun. We, the Coloured and native peoples of South Africa, have a tremendous fight before us. We have the war of wars to wage. No longer must we look to our friends in Great Britain. Our political destiny is in our hands and we must be prepared to face the fight with grim determination to succeed. "How are we to set about?" was the question. In our opinion, there is but one way and that is the economic method. Undoubtedly, the Coloured and the native races of South Africa hold the strongest weapon ever placed in the hands of any class. The very stability, the prosperity, even the continuance for but a few days of the economic existence of South Africa, depends on the labour market and we are the labour market. It may take long to come out that the necessity will be imposed on us, not in any isolation here and throughout the whole subcontinent to refuse to bolster up the economic fabric of the people who refuse us political freedom. That would bring the selfish white politicians to their knees. It would even show the white manual workers the value of combination, which is the only weapon whereby they will free themselves from the shackles of the system which is sapping the independence of the people within the nation, the national love of honour and increasing the severity and the extent of poverty for the production of a few sordid millionaires.' Though this scenario was probably not possible then, it shows the quality and thinking of black leadership at the time, especially the sense of unity among black people in South Africa.

As I have shown, the Congress Alliance of the later twentieth century was built on strong historical foundations. The unity of the African, Coloured and Indian people has been tempered in the heat of battle. In the early twentieth century the ANC was itself not a mass organisation; it only really became one when African women were allowed to join – a fact which is sometimes forgotten – and also after the formation of the Youth League in 1944. The early leaders of the Youth League included Anton Lembede, Mandela, Sisulu, A.P. Mda, Robert Sobukwe and others. In 1949, their Programme of Action was accepted by the ANC and committed that organisation to challenge white power. Much of the decision came from observing what Indian passive resisters had achieved in Natal in the late 1940s.

The Defiance Campaign of 1952 was also inspired and influenced, to some extent, by the Indian resistance campaign of the late 1940s. It involved cooperation between the ANC and the South African Indian Congress, building on the Xuma–Naicker–Dadoo Pact of 1947. The ANC and the Indian Congress as well as the Coloured People's Organisation and the (white) Congress of Democrats were also involved in the historic Congress of the People, which met in 1955 and adopted the Freedom Charter. The idea of the Congress of the People seems to have come from Professor Z.K. Matthews, president at the time of the Cape ANC. At a meeting he had declared: 'I wonder whether the time hasn't come for the African National Congress to consider the question of convening a national convention, a Congress of the People, representing all the people of this country, irrespective of race or colour, and to draw up a Freedom Charter for the democratic South Africa of the future. Once the principle of the establishment of such a Congress of the People was accepted, the details and its implementation could be worked out either by the National Executive, or by an ad hoc committee with that special duty.'

Out of the Congress came the Freedom Charter, a democratic vision of the future, which was to guide the ANC for the rest of the struggle. It would also feed into and animate the Constitution which the new democratic South Africa eventually adopted in 1996 after apartheid came to an end. Foremost among the statements within the Charter is the declaration that South Africa belongs to all who live in it, white and black. In giving expression to this, the ANC together with its partners in alliance affirmed its historical objective of uniting the people of South Africa as a whole and liberating black people, Africans in particular, from white oppression.

Ben Turok

Recently President Zuma has asked how we can create national unity around certain common ideals. Now this idea of creating national unity, even if at a very low level, was always in the eyes and the mind of the ANC, except that from its formation in 1912 until much later it was an Africans-only organisation. The question we have to ask ourselves is why that was the case, given the diversity of people in South Africa.

Firstly, let us look at what the main forces of our history were. After the discovery of gold and diamonds, tens of thousands – and then hundreds of thousands – of Africans were pushed out of the rural areas, and forced into the cities to work on the mines and in associated industries. This huge mass of African workers, at first very rural in their attitude, gradually became urbanised and started to organise themselves, for example, in the ICU and then in mineworkers' unions. In 1955 the South African Congress of Trade Unions (Sactu) was formed. So we see an African working class emerging as a result of the industrialisation of South Africa. This was the main force of what became the Congress Alliance.

But we also have to take account of the white workers. As Pallo Jordan has indicated, skilled British workers came out to South Africa to work on the mines. Many of them had been involved in unions in Britain, and when they arrived in South Africa they also organised unions on the mines. These British workers were joined by Afrikaner workers who had been driven off the land.

In 1922 English and Afrikaans workers rose in rebellion against an attempt by the mine owners to open skilled work to black labourers for lower wages. This led to the Rand Revolt. It was a real revolution, which was put down by military force, and a number of the workers were hanged for treason. So the working class was divided between, on the one side, African workers, and, on the other side, skilled white workers defending their privileges.

∩◯◯

I want to say a few words about the Communist Party. In 1915 white workers and East European socialists created the International Socialist League (ISL), which was typically European socialist in orientation. Then in 1921, inspired by the October Revolution in Russia, they formed the Communist Party of South Africa, led by white workers like Bill Andrews. They were a fairly small group and were concerned mainly with white worker issues. Radicalised by the Russian Revolution, some of them reacted against the more conservative white workers and their unions. In the late 1920s, under the influence of the Comintern, the international communist movement based in the Soviet Union, they adopted the policy of the Native Republic, or the Black Republic. Having originated from a conservative European labour tradition, they now underwent a big and contentious shift. The Communist Party became very active in the 1940s, especially among the mineworkers through people like J.B. Marks and Dan Tloome, who were communist leaders of the African Mineworkers' Union. The Party grew because of that militancy until it became so threatening to the white regime that in 1950 the National Party government banned it. At that time, the ANC, the Indian Congress and the Coloured People's Organisation were still legal, but the Communist Party was now driven underground.

So these were the forces at play at the beginning of the 1950s. What happened is that the dynamics of these different forces came together in the struggle against apartheid. The ANC, which was active in protesting against the banning of the Communist Party, realised that the National Party would in future ban it too, which is exactly what happened ten years later. This was a period of great political activity. In 1952 the ANC and the Indian Congress, drawn together by the Xuma–Naicker–Dadoo Pact, launched the Defiance Campaign, during which more than twenty thousand people were arrested. This created a real mass movement in South Africa. During the Defiance Campaign, many Indian, Coloured and white resisters as well as Africans went to prison – my wife too. She sat on a bench marked 'Non-Europeans only' in the Cape Town Post Office together with Albie Sachs and two other white students. We were not yet married, and I was standing there watching these four young people when a post office official came along and said, 'Hey, what are you doing here? *Jy kan nie daar sit nie. Dis vir Nie-Blankes.*' ('You cannot sit there. It is for non-whites.') So Albie Sachs, who was about 19 years old at the time, stood up and said, 'Sir, we are participating in the Defiance Campaign.' The official answered, *'Ag man, moenie nonsens praat nie'* ('Oh man, don't talk rubbish'). Albie responded, 'No sir, we are participating in the Defiance Campaign.' The official said, *'Ag*, you're mad' and walked away. They sat there for about half an hour, an hour, and nobody took any notice. Then the official came back and said, 'Listen, this is too much. We're going to call the police,' and Albie replied, 'Yes, sir. Please call the police, because we are defying.' So the police came and locked them up for a few hours.

It was this kind of action – the participation of Africans, Coloureds, Indians and a few democratic whites – that also led to the creation of the Congress of the People in 1955. Some two thousand delegates attended. I was privileged to be asked to speak and I introduced the economic clause. At the end of the second day the police stormed in with machine guns and went up to the platform. The chairman was smart and asked the police if he could close the congress. So he got up and said, 'Comrades, do you support – do you accept – the Freedom Charter?' and they all replied yes. That is how we succeeded in passing the Freedom Charter at the Congress of the People.

What was significant about the struggle of that time was that a new unity was built across racial lines. This unity was reinforced in the Treason Trial, which started about a year later, when 156 people of all races were arrested – there were about twenty-one whites, fifteen Indians, ten Coloureds and the rest Africans. We were all in court together; there were no racial barriers apart from the fact that the white accused were put in the white section of the Johannesburg Fort – people like Joe Slovo and Rusty Bernstein – while the Africans, Indians and Coloureds were put in the black section. But we met together in court as the Treason Trial accused. This sent out a wonderful message across the country that all races who believed in democracy could unite in the Congress Alliance. Such unity across racial lines was formalised in the joint executives of the Congress Alliance. What happened was that under the leadership of Chief Luthuli and the ANC, we all accepted that the Congress Alliance would be led by the ANC and by African leadership.

Personally, I have always believed that no matter the diversity and complexity of South African society, the struggle must be led by African leaders and by the ANC. This has been accepted throughout our history. At the Morogoro Conference in 1969, it was agreed that the main aspect of the struggle in South Africa was national liberation despite the emphasis placed by Marxists and communists on the pre-eminence of the class struggle. The ANC, and then the Congress Alliance, came to understand, as I think we understand today, that the main character of the struggle for liberation and democracy was the liberation of the black people, in particular the Africans, under African leadership.

So the Congress Alliance came together in the joint executives with ten delegates each from the ANC, the Indian Congress and the Coloured People's Organisation, and even ten delegates from the Congress of Democrats and from the Congress of Trade Unions – always under the leadership of Chief Luthuli. There was equality of representation despite the recognition that the main force of liberation was the African masses and that African leadership was essential as the main impetus of the struggle. The Treason Trial consolidated this. The fact that Indians and Coloureds and even some democratic whites were part of this was significant. The Treason Trial was no joke: there was in fact a time when the death sentence was thought to be certain. Yet we were all committed, all races, to the business of the struggle against the regime.

The year 1956 also witnessed the remarkable march by women on the Union Buildings, again led by representatives of the different races – Coloured, African, Indian and white. It was another attempt to make visible the non-racial character of the ANC and the movement. This concern of the movement to find a way of indicating non-racialism in practice remains today. It is not enough to rely on declarations that South Africa belongs to all who live in it, as the Freedom Charter states. There must be an element of visible unity among the races in South Africa. I can tell you, as a participant during the 1950s, that we made enormous efforts to demonstrate openly the multi-racial or non-racial character of the movement. I was a full-time activist in Cape Town at the time and whenever we held meetings in townships in Stellenbosch, Paarl and Worcester, we always ensured that there was an African leader or speaker, a Coloured and a white. We wanted to demonstrate to the people of South Africa that the ANC practised non-racialism. This is something we need to continue.

I cannot end without talking briefly about the formation of Umkhonto we Sizwe. MK deliberately included non-African cadres. When some of us were caught as MK cadres, the public of South Africa realised that sabotage could be carried out by Coloureds, Indians and even whites. This business of unity across racial lines in the struggle is important because the future of South Africa must include all races. We need to make the Freedom Charter a reality, visibly so, because there are people in the non-African communities who are also willing to struggle for a decent South Africa. Let us not ignore them. Let us rather bring them in and create an inclusive democracy.

Ten years ago if you went to an ANC conference in the Western Cape, people used to sing songs in Afrikaans, Xhosa and English, but no longer. In the past five years, at these conferences no Afrikaans songs have been sung. Comrades from the rural areas, from Paarl or Worcester, who come to a conference of the Western

Cape ANC, cannot participate because the proceedings are all in Xhosa. You see them sitting there, looking unhappy and alienated. In the province African people are a leading force, rightly so because they were the most disadvantaged historically, but the leading force must be inclusive.

I think that the ANC in the Western Cape has made huge mistakes by projecting an African image without worrying about Afrikaans, singing Afrikaans songs, without indicating even with tokenism and symbolism that Coloured people are important. Never mind whites, though it is also good to have the odd white symbolically. In the 1950s, by contrast, the movement was very careful to give an image of multi-racial leadership. We don't do that now at all. What is more, in the Western Cape the ANC has behaved as an exclusive club, and hence there has been a gradual disappearance of Coloured and white support.

In the Congress Alliance in the 1950s, we had no doubt at all that the ANC, which was then an Africans-only organisation, had to be the one that led the rest of the groups and gave a vision to its followers. So although as Indian, Coloured or white comrades you could offer your opinion and speak freely as equals, when it came to deciding critical issues about campaigns and policy, we all said the ANC must take the leading role. Today our African comrades still exercise leadership in the movement as a whole. The top six of the National Working Committee are all Africans. They have a responsibility to make others feel involved because they have the power. And so it depends on the leading people in the ANC to give leadership about non-racialism, to set the standard and offer a vision of inclusivity for the future.

ANTI-COLONIALISM

Adekeye Adebajo

There are four things that I want to do in this section. Firstly, I will provide a historical context for the international liberation struggle from the time of the Bandung Conference of 1955. Secondly, I will look at the role of some of the key figures in this 'Afro-Asian revolt against the West' – Gandhi, Nehru, Nkrumah and Nasser. Thirdly, I will examine the Non-Aligned Movement (NAM) and the United Nations; and finally, I will assess the legacy of the colonial struggle for contemporary international relations after the Cold War.

The year 2005 marked the fiftieth anniversary of a famous conference in the Indonesian city of Bandung. Here a diplomatic banquet took place at which Egypt's Gamal Abdel Nasser and India's Jawaharlal Nehru made common cause to establish the Non-Aligned Movement to challenge Western domination of the globe. This was the most symbolic event in the 'Afro-Asian revolt against the West', which unleashed the greatest change in the international system during the twentieth century, with the eventual decolonisation of two continents, Africa and Asia. The legacy of Bandung is thus the independence of Africa and Asia, which culminated in the end of apartheid by 1994. The decolonisation struggles were waged through the NAM, the United Nations, the Organisation of African Unity (now the African Union) and the Arab League. The NAM can, in a sense, be regarded as a political strategy to ward off foreign intervention in Afro-Asia, while the UN was the legal instrument to protect the newly won sovereignty of these states.

From the 1970s and throughout the 1980s, Bandung's legacy moved from being purely political to being economic. Ghana's Kwame Nkrumah had, of course, famously urged his fellow leaders to seek first the political kingdom and all other things would be added on to it. However, Nkrumah's political kingdom would eventually be replaced by Malaysian leader Mahathir Mohamad's economic kingdom as battles over equal terms of trade, redistribution of wealth, exploitative multinational corporations, and neo-colonial dependency took on a special urgency. The Organization of the Petroleum Exporting Countries (OPEC) challenged the international trading system by tripling oil prices in 1973. Many of these battles were spearheaded by the NAM. Just as Gandhi and Nkrumah had been symbols of the Afro-Asian political struggle, so Mahathir Mohamad became a symbol of the South's economic decolonisation. Mahathir championed an East Asian economic bloc as a 'caucus without the

Caucasians', as he called it, involving the Association of East Asian Nations (ASEAN) – Indonesia, Malaysia, Singapore, Brunei, Vietnam, Burma, Thailand, Laos and the Philippines – as well as China, Japan and Korea, but excluding the United States, Australia and New Zealand. By the 1990s, Mahathir's economic kingdom would be replaced by Thabo Mbeki's security kingdom. South Africa became the leading peacemaker and Nigeria the leading peacekeeper, in a decade of troubles after the Cold War.

Let us move now to the very beginning of the international liberation struggle. I start with the prophetic words of the father of pan-Africanism, W.E.B. Du Bois, who in 1900 famously and correctly predicted: 'The problem of the 20th century is the problem of the colour line, the relation of the darker to the lighter races of men in Asia and Africa, in America and the islands of the sea.' This was a remarkable prophecy, because by the end of the century, with the end of apartheid in South Africa, the decolonisation in Africa had been effectively completed, with the exception of Western Sahara.

European imperialism had reached its apogee at the start of the twentieth century. Between 1945 and 1960, altogether 40 African and Asian countries with populations of 800 million – over a quarter of the world's population at the time – had won their independence. Such a dramatic change in the international system had never occurred in world history. In Asia, Japan had shattered the myth of white invincibility through military victory over British, French and Dutch armies during the Second World War. These struggles had earlier antecedents. The Pan-African Congress was held simultaneously with the Paris Peace Conference, which ended the First World War in 1919, and called for the right of Africans to participate in their own governments. However, several of the early Pan-African Congresses actually dealt with social issues – social equality for Africans – rather than political issues and complemented the work of poets like Léopold Senghor and Aimé Césaire who called for, in a sense, *cultural* self-determination. The Indian National Congress' struggles were also spurred by Gandhi's return from South Africa to the Indian subcontinent in 1914; he organised the first mass mobilisation in India with his successful civil disobedience campaigns. The Mahatma's beliefs were to inspire seven Africans and Americans who would go on to win the Noble Peace Prize: Ralph Bunche, Albert Luthuli, Martin Luther King, Anwar Sadat, Desmond Tutu, Nelson Mandela and Barack Obama. With Gandhi's inspiration, Africa and Asia had changed the world from a Western-dominated one to a more truly international society. The Afro-Asians had humanised international diplomacy and given birth to the concept of non-alignment as a substitute for the destructive power politics that had lost Europe its global primacy and brought untold suffering to millions of people during Europe's two civil wars between 1914 and 1945, more commonly known as the First and Second World Wars.

A year before the Bandung Conference, Vietnamese freedom fighters had famously defeated France at Dien Bien Phu in 1954. The Vietnamese helped to blunt the prejudiced arrogance of Western powers by actually showing that non-Western countries could defeat militarily, not just France, but later the US too. I know that the African National Congress (ANC) drew a lot of inspiration from the Vietnamese liberation struggle and, indeed, visited their Vietnamese allies. Then, too, the resistance of Algerian freedom fighters to France's savage colonial war, which killed one million Algerians from 1954, also brought down the French Fourth Republic and laid the foundation for Algerian independence in 1962.

It must, however, be noted that the Afro-Asian bloc is not monolithic. Countries like China, Singapore and South Korea are today closer to joining the ranks of the international aristocratic Brahmins of the rich world. In contrast, many countries in the Third World belong to the group of international Dalits, the 'untouchables'. But Africa and Asia still have enough in common. Both were colonised by European powers on the basis of the ideologies of racial supremacy. Both have suffered from several wars, famines, military caudillos and autocrats; and both have struggled to evolve political and economic models based on the West, though adapted to local circumstances. Only Japan – the world's second largest economy – has, however, really been able to modernise without Westernising.

The Bandung Conference in 1955 expressed what Nehru described as 'the new dynamism of Asia and Africa'. Bandung sought to promote economic and cultural cooperation, support the decolonisation of Africa and Asia, promote world peace, and end racial discrimination and domination. It also sought to put an end to the 'politics of pigmentation' in which arrogant white statesmen set themselves up as overlords over local 'natives' who were considered unable to stand on their own feet in the difficult conditions of Western civilisation.

Three titanic figures towered over the southern landscape in this 'revolt against the West' – India's Nehru, who was the intellectual father of the concept of 'non-alignment' and had coined the phrase; Egypt's Nasser, who was the leader of pan-Africanism; and Ghana's Kwame Nkrumah, the most famous prophet of pan-Africanism. Nehru appeared to identify genuinely with Africa. He pushed strongly for the Non-Aligned Movement and the UN to support Africa's decolonisation efforts, and counselled African leaders against the dangers of one-party rule and military governments, though he was good friends with Egypt's military ruler, Nasser. He visited Nigeria, Sudan and Egypt in the early 1960s, and sought to rally the Afro-Asian coalition at the UN to support the anti-apartheid struggle, settle the Arab–Israeli dispute, and establish an Indian Ocean zone of peace. Nehru's controversial military annexation of the former Portuguese colony of Goa in 1961 helped to legitimise the use of armed force to liberate colonial territories. India's flamboyant Defence Minister, Krishna Menon, eloquently argued the case at the UN, declaring colonialism to be 'permanent aggression' in order to justify India's actions. During the Suez Crisis of 1956, Nehru helped to mobilise NAM support for Nasser. Like Gandhi, he exerted great influence on Nelson Mandela, who read Nehru's memoirs in prison and appropriately received the Nehru Award in 1980. Other African leaders, like Uganda's Milton Obote and Kenya's Jomo Kenyatta, also admired Nehru, and the Indian leader's ideals of non-alignment and embracing the Commonwealth without falling under the British Crown won support among many African leaders.

Nasser, who was a close ally of Nehru, staged the first military coup d'état in Africa in 1952. He was the foremost champion of pan-Africanism. He strongly backed Algerian independence from France and, like Nkrumah, the Egyptian leader championed 'positive neutrality'. He bought arms and received assistance from both East and West during the Cold War, and in his 1954 book *Philosophy of the Revolution*, he saw Egypt as being at the centre of three circles involving the Arab world, the Muslim world and Africa. However, his patronising offer of 'diffusing the light of civilization into the farthest parts of the virgin jungle' went down badly with many black Africans. It has been argued that, although Egypt's body is in Africa, its head and heart are really in the Middle East. Nasser was still acting as the 'gatekeeper of North Africa', as well as the political and cultural leader of the Arabian Peninsula. The most famous incident involving Nasser was the Suez Crisis of 1956, which led to a humiliating withdrawal of British and French forces. By ending the Anglo-French-Israeli take-over of the Canal, Nasser scored a famous political victory that added another sharp nail to the imperial coffin. The United States, at the time, supported the withdrawal of the British, French and Israelis, because it did not want such actions to push African and Asian countries into the arms of the Soviet Union during the Cold War.

The third of our 'terrible triplets', as I call them, Ghana's Kwame Nkrumah, was a disciple of Gandhi, and the Ghanaian leader's 'positive action' was clearly inspired by Gandhian methods of non-cooperation. Nkrumah argued that the independence of Ghana was meaningless unless it was linked with the total liberation of the African continent. In 1945 he helped to organise the fifth Pan-African Congress in Manchester, along with George Padmore. He then returned to Ghana to champion a brand of popular nationalism, using his formidable organisational skills to win his country's freedom. After gaining independence for Ghana in 1957, Nkrumah sought to keep the torch of pan-Africanism alive by promoting the independence of the entire continent. He proposed the idea of an African High Command as a common army to ward off external intervention in the continent. He called for a common currency, common foreign policy, even a political union with two parliamentary chambers. But Nkrumah was a visionary who was too far ahead of his time. At the time, most of Africa's leaders were still trying to turn their nations into states and consolidate their sovereignty. Nkrumah was also a fierce champion of non-alignment, sending Ghanaian troops to the UN mission in the Congo in 1960 in a bid to prevent the country from becoming a Cold War theatre. Like Thabo Mbeki, he was an African philosopher-king. Both of them were visionary intellectuals and pan-Africanists, probably the leading pan-African philosopher-kings of their generation.

The Non-Aligned Movement (NAM) was founded in 1961, six years after the Bandung Conference. Credit must go to Marshal Tito, president of Yugoslavia at the time, who was also considered one of the key 'founding fathers'. The NAM condemned imperialism in the Middle East and supported the Arabs in Palestine. The organisation suffered from the problem of trying to maintain unity among such a large and diverse group of states. The Sino-Soviet split and the border war between China and India in 1962 also shook the group's cohesion. Questions continued to be raised about how truly non-aligned Third World countries that hosted foreign bases on their territory could be. By the end of the Cold War, the NAM was suffering an identity crisis and critics asked what the group was non-aligned *against*.

The recent NAM summits in Malaysia (2003), Cuba (2006) and Egypt (2009) have seen the 118 members focusing more on issues of security, justice, democracy and sustainable development, as well as on how to implement the UN's Millennium Development Goals to halve poverty by 2015. Whereas concerns about foreign intervention had been paramount in the past, external neglect now seems to be the major concern.

It is important to acknowledge also the role of the UN in the Afro-Asian decolonisation struggle. Most, but not all, NAM members are part of the Group of 77 Developing Countries, set up in June 1964 in the context of the first UN Conference on Trade and Development (Unctad). The 130 countries of the G-77 and China, which continue to dominate the UN General Assembly's agenda, led many of these struggles, and the African Group, created in 1958, also played an important role. The Afro-Asians pushed forcefully for South Africa's suspension from the UN General Assembly in 1974, and pressured the 15-member UN Security Council to impose an arms embargo on the country in 1977, the first ever by the UN. The group also promoted the independence of Angola, Mozambique, Zimbabwe and Namibia. The unspoken Afro-Arab pact of the era involved the Africans supporting the Palestinian cause in exchange for the Asians and the Arabs supporting the anti-apartheid struggle, as well as decolonisation efforts on the continent.

In conclusion, it is important to identify ways of rekindling the 'spirit of Bandung' so as to foster greater Afro-Asian cooperation in future. Generally, Asia has done better economically than Africa in the first fifty years of independence, and several Asian states have joined the ranks of the *nouveaux riches*. The Asian financial crisis of 1997–8, however, highlighted the region's continued vulnerability to Western financial actors and demonstrated the fragility of the 'Asian miracle'. The New International Economic Order (NIEO) promoted by Afro-Asian leaders in the 1970s proved, in the end, to be a tragic illusion and mirage. Instead, the 'global South' found itself after the Cold War in an age of the neo-liberal 'Washington Consensus' of free markets and a limited role for the state. More recently, the global financial crisis of 2007–9 has forced a reassessment of this market fundamentalism, as it has been clearly demonstrated that the magic of the market distributes its rewards very unevenly. Africa's share of global trade has declined from about 6 per cent in the early 1980s to only 2 per cent in 2006, and, as US Secretary of State Hillary Clinton noted during a recent visit to the region, Africa is the only continent that does not trade 'internally' very well.

Most of the sub-regional groups in Africa conduct less than 10 per cent of their trade among themselves, but Africa increasingly supplies Asia with its oil and other resources. By 2008, Asia was consuming 40 per cent of the world's oil. South Africa has strong trade ties with East Asia, Japan, China and India. Japan, China and India have also recently come up with initiatives on Africa, while Beijing has become the third largest foreign investor on the continent after the US and Europe. By 2006, China's bilateral trade with Africa had reached $55 billion. Therefore, it is important for Africa to look for ways of actually using this leverage to negotiate improved terms of trade with the West. Powerful Western governments also continue to prefer to exert their influence through the World Bank, the International Monetary Fund (IMF), and the World Trade Organisation (WTO) rather than through the UN. In 2008, Washington and its European allies still had 53 per cent of the voting shares in the IMF, while sub-Saharan Africa had only two executive directors on a 24-member IMF and World Bank board. South Africa has consistently pushed for the restructuring of these global financial institutions.

Before the Group of 20 meeting in London in April 2009, Brazilian President Luiz Inácio Lula da Silva, a man from a poor working-class background, caused a storm by saying that the global financial crisis of 2007–9 had been caused by 'blue-eyed white men with blond hair' who had arrogantly, he implied, seen themselves as 'masters of the universe'. Across the Third World, the 'non-white' three-quarters of the world's population perfectly understood Lula's words, though much of the Western media was aghast at this lack of political correctness from a global statesman. However, the fact that the most powerful man at the G-20 summit was Barack Obama, an Afro-Saxon US president with a Kenyan father who has recently been awarded the Nobel Peace Prize, seemed to vindicate Lula. The fact that China, the new 'workshop of the world', is now the world's third-largest economy – and three of the five largest banks in the world are Chinese – is further proof of the shift in the global balance of power. The London summit of April 2009 was forced to agree to discuss an end to the 65-year system of 'global apartheid,' according to which an American always heads the World Bank and a European always heads the IMF. The weighted voting that allows mostly rich Western countries to dominate both Bretton Woods Institutions must also come to a speedy end, and other countries must make their voices heard so that the 'spirit of Bandung' can finally prevail.

PAN-AFRICANISM

Mathole Motshekga

Pan-Africanism has made a substantial contribution to the evolution of ANC policy. Even today, it is still relevant. The reason for this is that, in my view, the national question has not yet been resolved. We are still suffering from the legacy of slavery and colonialism, with the result that we have class, gender and other social cleavages and divisions in our country. We also have not even reached a consensus about the values that should animate our society. According to the ANC's 'Strategy and Tactics' document of 2007, our aim is to build a united, democratic society in which the value of all citizens is measured by our common humanity. Under conditions of slavery and colonialism, ordinary people's humanity was not recognised. That we are still talking about the need to recover our humanity means that we still recognise that the legacy of slavery and colonialism continues to exist and must be dealt with.

If there is one goal above all that we want to achieve, it is to build a nation that is socially cohesive. Let us compare, for the moment, our situation on the African continent and the position of slaves in the Americas.

The people who were taken into slavery came from different parts of the continent, speaking different languages and observing different cultures. Yet once in captivity in America it was possible for these people, without being literate in the modern sense, to recognise that they had a human worth that would not allow them to submit to indignity. As a result, some of them ran away and established new communities. When they and their descendants found themselves discriminated against in the churches, they withdrew and set up their own churches and schools, forming new communities which were cohesive.

What is interesting is that, unlike in our case, where we are still debating whether a Coloured is an African or who is included in the term 'black', if you look at the descendants of the slaves in America, some are brown, others are black, but they are all clear that they are African Americans. Their solidarity is apparent and they are able to develop freely because they have resolved the question of identity, which I think we have not yet resolved.

One of the original purposes of the ANC was to bring together a wide variety of different ethnic groups and tribes, to bring about unity and cooperation between people of colour, yet we are still grappling with the issue of identity. In my view we need to pursue the pan-African ideal because it is a tool that we can use for nation building and social cohesion.

When we look at the basis for cohesion among black people in the Americas, it is derived from African culture itself, which I describe as the disposition to unite for mutual benefit. This is what the slaves benefited from. We have something to learn from the situation in the United States. If we can only unite as South Africans across colour and tribe, we will benefit greatly and develop rapidly.

In the Americas, there were objective conditions that made people come together and form communities, such as discrimination in the churches and oppression in the workplace. These objective conditions helped the slaves and their descendants to develop a social, and even a political, consciousness. The other factor that made for cohesion came from religion itself. When slaves read the Bible, they came across a verse in Psalm 68 which read: 'Ethiopia shall soon stretch out her hands unto God'. In their interpretation, 'Ethiopia' meant the whole of Africa and the verse both reminded them of past glories and assured them of glories to come if they resisted oppression. Again, the eighth chapter of the Acts of the Apostles records the conversion of a eunuch of Ethiopia by an apostle of Jesus. To the slaves this indicated that their affiliation with the Christian religion reached far back to apostolic times and preceded in fact the conversion of Europe to Christianity and the impact of European missionary work in Africa. All of this gave them a sense of pride and self-worth. From it developed the cluster of ideas referred to as Ethiopianism, which was both a theological position and a national or rather pan-national identity. Many of these ideas were taken up and spread by the African Methodist Episcopal (AME) Church, the first independent African-American church in the United States. The AME began missionary activities in South Africa in the late 1890s. Very soon a succession of AME bishops was sent out to South Africa to superintend the growing church there.

The influence that Ethiopianism had on South Africa and the ANC in particular was brought about by the fact that many young South Africans went to the United States at the turn of the twentieth century to study. Charlotte Maxeke, who later founded the predecessor of the ANC Women's League, studied at Wilberforce University, an AME foundation. Here she was taught and inspired by the African-American scholar and politician W.E.B. Du Bois, 'the father of pan-Africanism', who believed that the struggles of black people everywhere were inseparable. On her return to South Africa, Maxeke founded the Wilberforce Institute at Evaton on the Witwatersrand. She and her husband also worked for the AME in South Africa. Similarly, while a student in the United States, John Dube, founding president of the ANC, was inspired by the famous educational institution at Tuskegee, Alabama, that had been set up by Booker T. Washington, the leading African-American spokesman of the time; and on his return to South Africa, Dube established the Ohlange Institute in Natal.

Modern pan-Africanism began to establish itself at

the beginning of the twentieth century and soon found its way to South Africa. In 1900 a Pan-African Congress was held in London. After the conference, its organiser, Henry Sylvester Williams, a Trinidadian-born advocate, came to Cape Town and spread the message of black race pride there. Williams became one of the founding members of the African People's Organisation or APO, which developed into the leading Coloured political organisation in South Africa. Among its principal aims were those of promoting 'unity between the coloured [i.e. black] races' and 'the general advancement of the coloured [i.e. black] people in South Africa'. These aims make apparent the influence of pan-Africanism on the APO.

The early influence of pan-Africanism on the ANC can be traced through the biography of Sol Plaatje, the first secretary-general of the organisation. In 1919, at the end of the First World War, Du Bois convened a Pan-African Congress in Paris, hoping to draw the attention of the delegates to the Versailles Peace Conference to the rights of black people. When notice of the congress was sent out to African, West Indian and African-American political organisations, the ANC decided to send a deputation. But funds could not be raised in time, and the ANC was in the end not among the organisations represented at the congress. Nevertheless, Sol Plaatje, who had planned to attend the congress, remained in touch with Du Bois and a speech by Plaatje on the effects of the Natives Land

Act was read out at a subsequent Pan-African Congress that Du Bois convened in 1921. This congress was also attended by John Dube.

Another strong pan-African influence on black South Africans came from the ideas of Marcus Garvey, the president and driving force of the Universal Negro Improvement Association. Though based in the United States, the Association spread to every part of the world, with the aim of uniting black people everywhere. With its millennial undertones, Garveyism foresaw the day of Africa's liberation. After the First World War, the Garvey movement, also known as the 'Africa for the Africans' movement, developed in South Africa as a powerful form of mass-based African nationalism. There were branches in Pretoria, Kimberley, Johannesburg, Cape Town and Durban. It had a strong influence on the thinking of Josiah Gumede, who was elected ANC president in 1927 and who also showed strong leanings towards the Communist Party.

In 1945 many of the strands I have considered came together in the famous Pan-African Congress held in Manchester. It was attended by Garvey's widow, Kwame Nkrumah and many others. This congress provided the impetus for the movement for African independence after the Second World War. Within a few decades of the congress many former colonies in Africa gained their freedom from colonial rule and set up independent nation states. In my view, the promise of their foundation has not been fulfilled and many of them cannot cohere. There are different reasons for this, but it is my feeling that pan-Africanism needs to be revisited, developed and used as a tool to build these young nations and make them cohesive. At the centre of our problems as African states lies a crisis in values. I believe that pan-Africanism can make a contribution to the recovery of our humanity and of the values needed to create cohesive societies.

MARXISM

Ben Turok

In this section I want to discuss, firstly, the general theory of society from a Marxist viewpoint because Marxism developed as a theory of society – not just of classes, but of society as a whole. Secondly, I will say something about why Marxism emerged. Then I will talk about Marxism and imperialism, or Marxism in the modern period of imperialism, because Marxism started before imperialism. Fourthly, as Marxism was developed in the industrial countries of Europe, I will discuss the democratic and socialist revolutions and the link between the two.

Let us begin with the general theory of society according to Marx. Marx was a brilliant philosopher, a follower of the German philosopher Hegel, who then turned to economics. He linked up with Friedrich Engels and the two of them began to analyse capitalism in Germany, England and the rest of Europe. They tried very hard to be scientific in their approach. What they tried to do, like any scientist, was to analyse the general laws of society and the way society develops, using the idea of modes of production through the succeeding eras of slavery, feudalism, capitalism and so on. While they attempted to develop general laws of society scientifically, the main concentration or focus was on capitalism. Marx's argument went along these lines: An owner of money buys a factory. He buys machines and raw materials, and those machines and that factory sit there. Nothing happens. Then he gets a worker or workers. They come to the factory. The worker begins to work on the goods, on the raw materials, and uses the machines and suddenly you have goods. Before the worker labours, there are no goods. So for example, you have a factory, machinery and timber. Nothing happens until a worker arrives. He begins to work on the timber using the machinery. Suddenly, you get furniture.

So Marx's theory of economics states clearly that the way value is created in society is through the worker. The worker's labour creates value. Without the worker, there is no value.

The interesting thing is that before Marx, the bourgeois economist Adam Smith also elaborated a labour theory of value. What Marx did was to develop this in the three volumes of *Capital*, and add something that is a distinctive contribution. Marx said that when the worker produces goods, value is created, but the worker does not receive the full value. He only gets a part of the value. The surplus value – today we talk about profit – is taken by the employer. This is the basis of Marx's economic theory – that workers through their labour create value. The employer takes a part, which is the surplus value, and the worker receives a wage. This is the basic theory of capitalism.

Now as the workers become stronger and more organised, they begin to struggle over wages. In other words, they struggle for a bigger share of value. This is the basis of the class struggle. But the class struggle is not only over wages – though here some Marxists, including South African Marxists, get it wrong. They say that Marxism is a question of struggle between workers and employers. It *is* that – a struggle over wages – but it is also a bigger struggle, a struggle over the institutions of capitalism. What Marx said was that the relations of production are never simply economic relations; there are other issues. We in South Africa know that in the past the struggle of workers against employers included the pass laws and all kinds of other oppressive legislation because the workers' struggle against employers could never succeed unless they also tackled the whole structure of apartheid. This proved that the theories of Marx were correct. Class struggle is about the relations of production, including the superstructure of the state, its laws and so on. That is why when the workers struggle for wages, they also struggle for democracy.

It is in this context that people began to ask questions about what was wrong with the capitalist system. So socialism began to emerge among workers and intellectuals because they recognised that the system of capitalism was deeply flawed and that a better society could be envisaged. Marx and Engels wrote *The Communist Manifesto* as a manifesto of socialist ideas.

Of course, the moment that class struggle begins – and class struggle includes the laws and parliament – the ruling class starts to defend itself. Marx said that in every society the ruling class will defend its institutions of exploitation and oppression. So they use parliament and all the institutions of law, the judiciary and the police, to set up a protective mechanism to defend their power. The struggle is not just about wages. It is about the laws, parliament, the judiciary, culture, the churches – it is about every single institution you can think of. Suddenly, what started off as a struggle between workers and employers in a factory becomes a huge struggle about the future of society. That is the basic message of Marxism.

Let me say something about why Marxism grew. What happened in Europe is that, as it industrialised, so the proletariat grew in size and in power. Workers began to organise in trade unions. The same thing happened in South Africa. As the mining industry grew, the African proletariat grew and an African working class developed. They began to reject the values of exploitation and oppression and to talk about solidarity and equality, about human values, the worth of a human being, about quality of life. Suddenly the whole discussion develops a profundity which goes way beyond wages. Of course, you never lose the wages issue but the struggle around capitalism for socialism has a philosophical depth which is far greater than just wage demands. Later, Lenin and others began to talk about global capitalism because capitalism spread very fast from Germany and England to the whole of Europe and then to the United States.

Now in the modern era, after the Russian Revolution, the Soviet Union emerged and introduced a command economy. At first, this was very successful. The Soviet Union industrialised very fast until certain atrophies set in and the command economy froze; similar problems arose in all the communist-led countries in Eastern Europe, leading to a crisis and, ultimately, collapse.

In the United Kingdom, the capitalist class realised it had a problem because the trade union movement, represented in Parliament by the Labour Party, was very strong. What the capitalists did was to buy off the British working class by paying them higher wages, giving them rights to join unions, and paid for this by exploiting the colonies. By exploiting Africa, Latin America, China and India – and deriving super-profits – they were able to pay British workers more. The same thing happened in South Africa. South African mining and industrial companies employed African labour and used that sweated profit to pay white workers more. They divided the working class in South Africa along race lines. The white working class was highly organised. During the 1922 Rand strike, the capitalists bought off the white mineworkers with higher pay and better conditions at the expense of African labour. That is why we said that South Africa was colonialism of a special type because the oppressor and the exploited existed in the same country.

Let us look at Marxism as a world movement. In the mid-twentieth century we find an interesting development. In 1944–5, during the Second World War, Eastern Europe was taken over by Soviet forces and communist regimes were introduced – some would say imposed – in East Germany, Hungary, Poland and elsewhere. The whole of Eastern Europe fell under communist control. Even in France and Italy, the Communist Party grew strong during the war and after. Then in 1949 there was the success of the Chinese Revolution. Mid-century, one-third of the world was under Communist Party rule, including Cuba. When I joined the movement the period was one of enormous victories and things looked very rosy with a large part of the world under progressive rule.

Marxism as a world movement declined very rapidly, however. We need to analyse this to understand why, because in South Africa there are many – the Communist Party and Cosatu – who say the objective remains socialism. As for the ANC, it is not a socialist movement. As Pallo Jordan has remarked, the ANC's policy is inclusive African nationalism.

I need to say something at this point about primitive accumulation, which was one of the theories that Marx propounded. What this means is that usually under capitalism there are capitalists and workers. When capitalism and industrialisation first developed in England, there were farm labourers and tenants on the land. What the English ruling class did was to introduce 'Enclosure Acts', which deprived them of their land and forced them to go and work in the factories. The same thing happened in South Africa. Here the capitalist class also used taxes, land restrictions and, above all, the Land Act to force black workers to work in the mines and in industry. According to Marx, this is not normal capitalism but primitive accumulation, because it involves coercion, forced labour and dispossession in order to create an urban proletariat, which is the army of labour.

In 1917 Lenin wrote an important book, *Imperialism: The Highest Stage of Capitalism*, because by his time capitalism had changed. Instead of being confined to single countries like Britain, Germany and France, capitalism had spread into the colonies. Something new had happened. In Lenin's analysis, finance capital (the banks) and industrial capital had combined into one and become a powerful force in Europe and the United States. This very rich class began to penetrate and control the Third World – Africa, Asia and Latin America – and this led to a new economic relationship between the industrial world and the colonies. Of course, the process also led to the emergence of national liberation movements and independence movements. In Latin America, many countries gained independence from Europe in the nineteenth century, but despite their independence neo-colonialism gained hold of them and there was no real fundamental change.

The analysis of neo-colonialism is very important. Neo-colonialism happened right across Africa – in Nigeria, Ghana and Kenya, as elsewhere – as Nkrumah and others observed. So we must ask the question: 'If the structure in South Africa was once colonialism of a special type, is it still colonialism of a special type?' I still have some questions about this in my own mind. If it is colonialism of a special type, are we moving into neo-colonialism in the way that Nigeria, Ghana and Latin America have? Neo-colonialism means that there is a comprador class of indigenous people which collaborates with the colonial class. We need to ask, as some are asking in Cosatu and the Communist Party, if a parasitic comprador class is now emerging in South Africa, performing a function not very different from the neo-colonial class in Africa and Latin America.

The argument is sometimes made, especially by left-wing intellectuals and some African intellectuals, that South Africa today is a sub-imperialist power on the African continent. According to Lenin and Marx, imperialism is a total system of subjugation and control. I do not think that South Africa today controls the rest of Africa. It may be investing in and even exploiting parts of the rest of Africa, but not every country that invests in another is imperialist. Imperialism is a particular phenomenon, a historical phenomenon, and we should not confuse it with business investment and exploitation.

Finally, we need to look at the relation between national revolution and social revolution. The interesting thing is that in Russia the Communist Party fought for the Democratic Revolution in March 1917 and the Socialist Revolution in October 1917. In other words, what happened in Russia was a two-stage process. Similarly, in China, there was an anti-feudal revolution led by Chiang Kai-shek in 1911, and then the anti-imperialist revolution in 1949: two stages once again. The question for South Africa is whether we will also proceed through a two-stage revolution. The ANC, in its 'Strategy and Tactics' document of 2007, is very clear and unequivocal about the fact that we are fighting a National Democratic Revolution to build a democratic society. But Cosatu says that we must use the tools of Marxism and Leninism and fight for socialism, while the Communist Party is also fighting for socialism under the banner of Marxism and Leninism.

During the period of exile there was a lot of discussion about this question of two stages or one, and there were different views. Joe Slovo, who was the main theorist at the time, once said that because the proletariat in South Africa was highly organised, large and revolutionary, and there was no middle stratum worth talking about, the contradictions were too strong. Slovo held the view that if the ANC could effect the Democratic Revolution, it would move into the Socialist Revolution. There would be a steady change in that way. Today I think it is still an open question. Where is the ANC going to be in twenty or thirty years' time? Are we going to be a social democracy? Cosatu does not think so, nor does the Communist Party. They want socialism. All this is still undecided and uncharted territory.

SOCIAL DEMOCRACY

Febe Potgieter-Gqubule

I am going to deal with the historical background to the evolution of social democracy. Then I will look at some of its theoretical foundations and its main principles and values, before concluding with a look at its impact on the ANC.

My starting point is the ANC's 2007 'Strategy and Tactics' document, in which the ANC referred for the first time to social democracy by name. In the document we read: 'The ANC therefore seeks to build democracy with social content. Informed by our own concrete conditions and experiences, this will, in some respects, reflect elements of the best traditions of social democracy, which include a system which places the needs of the poor and social issues such as health care, education and a social safety net at the top of the national agenda; intense role of the state in economic life; pursuit of full employment; quest for equality; strong partnership with the trade union movement; and promotion of international solidarity.'

What are the historical roots of social democracy? If one looks at the social democratic movement, it is based mainly in Europe, so when we talk about social democracy, we are referring to Western Europe in particular. While some aspects of social democracy can be found historically in South American parties, the mass parties on that continent fall more within the tradition of Marxism. In South America social democratic parties tend to be predominantly middle class, small in size and enjoying very little electoral support, although they do tend to work with mass organisations that are oriented more towards workers.

Some of the roots of social democracy go back to the beginnings of capitalism. This period saw the rejection of feudalism and the emergence of liberalism, which argued that capitalism was the great advance that would lead to the destruction of the feudal system. This would enable the new class of the bourgeoisie to make money and to expand production, and workers to be 'free' to sell their labour. Liberalism argued that all we need to do is to make sure that everybody is free; and by 'freedom' was meant the right to sell one's labour.

In the early nineteenth century socialism developed as a rejection of the harshest effects and conditions of the Industrial Revolution, for example child labour. Working people during this time laboured in terrible circumstances and lacked the freedom promised by liberalism. This led to a critique of capitalism as a form of enslavement of workers and the emergence of utopian socialism.

When Marx and Engels began to develop their

theories, they acknowledged that capitalism was a great transforming force that had helped break up feudalism. However, they also showed the inherent contradictions at the heart of capitalism – how it produces wealth and productivity, but based on terrible inequality, exploitation and conflict.

During the course of the nineteenth century, there grew up all over Europe workers' parties, based on the trade union movement that had begun to organise in factories around working conditions and wages and against child labour. Towards the end of the century two strands began to emerge within the socialist movement – revolutionary socialism and social democracy – although both of these considered themselves as having their roots in Marxism. The revolutionary socialists basically argued that the capitalist system was compromised and couldn't be reformed. Only a revolution could overthrow the political and economic system of capitalism and replace it with the power of the workers and the proletariat, and put in place a new economic and social order based on equality and freedom from poverty. This trend within the socialist movement also argued that the state is simply a representative of class interests. As the state within capitalist societies is a bourgeois state, it did not make sense for socialists to work within it to effect its transformation.

The second strand, which developed around people like Lassalle and the Fabian Society in Britain, talked of the improvement of workers' conditions, within the context of the capitalist system. The question they posed was how best to use the expansion of parliamentary democracy taking place at the time through the extension of the vote to men and, later, women. According to this view, the state was a tool that could be used to begin to address social conditions in society, particularly working conditions for workers. Society could be improved and ameliorated by passing laws to outlaw child labour, for example, or introducing a minimum wage or better working conditions. Advocates of this strand argued that it was important for socialists to work within the system to improve conditions for workers, and not merely wait for the collapse or destruction of the capitalist state and capitalist economic system. They believed that it was possible for socialism to build a mixed economy, with both private property and state property, even at the level of municipalities and local government. If you look at the German system today, you can see that even the local governments have large stakes in banks and various companies. These people were referred to as 'reform socialists' or 'social democrats'.

They also questioned some of the fundamental assumptions of Marxism – that once capitalism develops to a certain point it will reach a crisis and either destroy itself or, with a push from the working class, be destroyed. Their understanding of capitalism was that it was a very complex system, that it had developed through different crises and that it had the ability to adapt itself. Being committed to equality and social justice they felt they needed to work within the system and take the struggle forward, rather than wait for the magic moment of crisis that would topple the system.

The final issue that set them aside from the revolutionary socialists was their belief that the state does not necessarily represent the dominant classes of the productive system. If you look at the state at any point in time, it is contested. While it may serve the interests of a particular class, because of the extension of the franchise the state also has a responsibility to act (or at least *appear* to act) as the representative of the interests of other people (the workers, the middle class, the poor and so on).

In the remainder of this chapter, I am going to focus on how social democracy developed and came to influence our policies and approaches today.

Both strands that I have examined worked together in the Second International, but eventually the Second International collapsed because of differences about the role of the state, parliament and trade unions in fighting for workers' rights under the capitalist system. There was vigorous debate within the Second International about these issues. Rosa Luxemburg, for one, wrote a book, *Reform and Revolution*, in which she critiqued the social democratic approaches to these issues.

Two key developments in the twentieth century brought things to a head. When the First World War broke out, the revolutionary socialists argued that it was an imperialist war and socialists should have nothing to do with it. On the other hand, the social democrats argued that the war involved broader issues, such as democracy and national sovereignty, and they joined the war effort in their respective countries.

The second development that led to the split of the movement was the Bolshevik Revolution in 1917. One of the propositions of early Marxism was that, according to the theory of historical materialism, socialism grows out of or bursts forth from within the womb of capitalism. There is an assumption about a certain level of development that is necessary before you can reach the next stage. In 1917 the Bolshevik Revolution took place in a relatively 'backward' country in terms of capitalist development and industrialisation – Russia was still largely feudal in character. This anomaly caused a big split within the socialist movement – with some disagreeing about whether Russia was 'ready' for a socialist revolution, according to traditional Marxism, and others questioning the use of violence and other issues around democracy.

After the collapse of the Second International, the two strands split up and went their separate ways. On the one hand, there were those who supported the developments in Russia (and eventually the Soviet Union) and, on the other hand, there were the social democrats, mainly in Western Europe.

The 1930s saw the Great Depression and a huge crisis for capitalism. Once again the socialist movement confronted the question of how to respond. Many social democrats were beginning to participate in Parliament, as part of coalition governments; some were even in power. Should they try to introduce policies that would contribute towards the improvement of workers' rights under capitalism or should they join hands with revolutionary socialism to deliver the final push to the capitalist system?

Let me say here that both strands within socialism shared a commitment to social justice and equality. What they disagreed about was their analysis of society and of the strategy and tactics needed to bring about equality and social justice. This had major implications for their programmes and the adoption of appropriate strategies to achieve their goals.

The 1930s and the Great Depression led to the emergence of three broad political movements in Europe. The first was the rise of fascism in Germany, Italy and elsewhere. The second was social democracy and its consolidation. The third was 'real existing socialism'. After the Second World War, social democrats in Europe affirmed the primacy of politics over the economy. In their view, the way to establish a society with greater equality, in which to address issues of poverty and create better working conditions, was to ensure that the political structure had dominance over the economic system. That is what social democracy, especially in Western Europe, tried to do – to put in place the welfare state, with generous social security benefits in terms of housing, childcare, unemployment insurance, pensions, the social wage, free education, free health care and so on. They funded this through taxation of companies and the rich, and used these resources to establish a system of redistribution through the development of the welfare state. It is somewhat ironic that some of the countries that used these policies to assist reconstruction after the Second World War have advised against similar policies in helping reconstruct South Africa after apartheid because 'they don't work'.

Turning to our own history, we should note that early in the twentieth century the South African Labour Party was formed to look after the interests of mainly white workers and miners. Like much of the labour movement at the time, the Labour Party was unashamedly racist, opposing the employment of 'natives' in skilled jobs and the further immigration of Indians to South Africa. At the beginning of the First World War the Labour Party split on the question of whether to support the British war effort. From the split emerged the International Socialist League, forerunner of the Communist Party of South Africa (CPSA), which was established in 1921 and which was itself the precursor of the SACP.

Since the early 1960s there have been fraternal relations between European social democrats and the southern African liberation movements. Olof Palme, leader of the Swedish Social Democratic Party and Sweden's prime minister, and Willy Brandt, German chancellor and leader of the Social Democratic Party in his country, both played an important role in supporting the liberation movements in southern Africa. During the struggle years the ANC had observer status within the Socialist International while the youth movements had observer status in the International Union of Socialist Youth.

What have been the theoretical developments in social democratic thinking in South Africa? The ANC's 'Strategy and Tactics' document of 2007 talks mainly about social democracy in its political sense, in terms of parliamentary democracy, civil rights and so on. I think it is important from the point of view of theory to argue that you can improve people's lives – through ameliorating working conditions, redistribution and the radical ways pursued in Scandinavian countries – within the context of a democracy. You don't have to have a one-party state. You can improve people's lives in a plural political system in which civil rights are recognised and protected. However, it is also important to establish a relation between political rights, with which liberalism has been mostly concerned, and socio-economic rights. If you look at the Freedom Charter, you can see that a balance has been struck between these two legs. On the one hand the people shall govern, but at the same time all shall be equal before the law. Similarly, the land belongs to those who work it, but the people shall also share in the country's wealth. So the Charter strikes a balance between political rights and socio-economic rights and acknowledges that you can't have the one without the other. You need to have a combination of the two.

China provides an interesting case study in this respect. In many ways China's approach mirrors much of what social democracies attempted after the Second World War – such as the strong directing role played by the state within the economy to decide on what industries to support in order to draw more people into the labour force. A major difference is that, unlike the social democracies of Western Europe, China's industrial policy occurs at the expense of the working people, who earn very low wages and endure poor working conditions. This is a challenge that South Africa faces today. One of the reasons for China's situation is that it does not have a strong independent trade union movement. All of the social democratic parties in Europe came into power on the back of strong labour movements, which agreed to temper their demands and refrain from going out on strike, so as to make their economies attractive for investment, in return for state protection of their rights, decent wages and so on. That is why a strong trade union movement is so important to ensure a social contract of this kind that balances economic growth with social justice.

Let us now turn to the question of international solidarity. In 1980, Willy Brandt, who was president of the Socialist International for many years, chaired the Commission for International Developmental

Issues, popularly known as the Brandt Commission. The commission developed the concept of North versus South and argued that in the world today we have a division between the relatively wealthy and developed North and the poor and undeveloped South. This division is partly the product of the history of colonialism but also reflects the unequal relationship that has developed in the global economic system. In response to this division between North and South in the globalised world, it becomes imperative for social democrats to make use of international solidarity. If capital has become international and multinational, then labour must, too, and align itself with progressive movements worldwide.

There is a very good recent example from Africa. A South African retail chain opened up in Zambia and wanted to pay workers in their stores what it called 'Zambian' wages. It argued that the chain couldn't pay South African wages because Zambia was not at the same level of development. So the workers in Zambia linked up with the South African retail workers' union Saccawu (the South African Commercial Catering and Allied Workers' Union) and asked for assistance and information about the retail chain's financial statements, profit margins and so on. Armed with this information, Zambian workers could organise for better wages through their link with Saccawu in South Africa.

In conclusion, let us look at the fortunes of social democracy in the era of globalisation after 1990. At the time when the ANC came to power in 1994, the socialist bloc of states in Eastern Europe had collapsed and a unipolar world had emerged. Neo-liberalism was ascendant and triumphant while social democracy seemed to be in retreat. People in many countries were beginning to ask whether the welfare state could be sustained, whether free education was possible for everybody, whether the current national health care system could be maintained and whether people could continue to enjoy generous unemployment benefits. These questions were raised in the context of a globalised world where big companies and businesses no longer had the same kind of loyalty to national development that marked the post-world war era. In the UK, under the Labour Party, and in several other European countries, owing to the pressures of globalisation there has been a retreat from the principles of social justice and inequality. In Sweden and Denmark, by contrast, the response has been an acknowledgement of the need for the state to intervene to protect the interests of working people and the living standards of the majority of people.

In addition, there were changes in the labour market during the early 1990s as industrial production moved from Europe and America to other parts of the world, such as China, the Philippines and Indonesia. All of a sudden, countries such as Sweden found themselves with the unusual crisis of an unemployment problem. In Sweden, as a result, social democrats were voted out of power for the first time in thirty years.

I think the ANC is at present having to deal with many of the same issues faced by social democratic parties in Europe during the 1990s and after. If one looks at the labour market today – with its problems of outsourcing and various forms of casualisation – what should the state do to protect workers' rights? While neo-liberals argue that we should not tax business but create a 'friendly' environment for its operation, how does the state ensure that, at the same time as providing sufficient resources to support industrial policy, it can provide social benefits to the working people? This is a key part of the challenge that we face.

The final point I want to make, which is relevant for the ANC, is the issue of the 'retreat of politics' that has characterised the era of globalisation since the early 1990s. This situation pertains across the world, and not just in South Africa. Whenever politicians or ministers speak, their first concern is with the markets and investors and only then do they think of their own constituency. Social democrats have everywhere been grappling with the issue of how to reassert the primacy of politics over economics, and it is an issue which the ANC faces as well in South Africa.

Chronology

1912 ANC founded

1920 ICU formed

1921 Communist Party of SA established

1922 Rand Revolt

1943 'Africans' Claims' issued by ANC

1944 ANC Youth League established

1945 Anti-pass campaign

1946 African mineworkers' strike

1947 Xuma–Naicker–Dadoo pact

1949 ANC adopted Programme of Action

1950 Communist Party banned

1952 Defiance Campaign

1953 Congress of Democrats and Coloured People's Organisation founded

1955 Congress of the People adopted the Freedom Charter

1956 Treason Trial commenced

1956 Women's march on Union Buildings

1960 Sharpeville Massacre and banning of ANC

1961 Umkhonto we Sizwe (MK) formed

1963 Rivonia Trial commenced

1969 ANC Special Conference, Morogoro

1985 ANC National Conference, Kabwe

1990 ANC and SACP unbanned

1991 ANC National Conference, Durban; Mandela elected president

1994 First democratic elections

1997 ANC National Conference, Mafikeng

2000 ANC National General Council, Port Elizabeth

2002 ANC National Policy Conference, Kempton Park

2002 ANC National Conference, Stellenbosch

2005 ANC National General Council, Pretoria

2007 ANC National Conference, Polokwane

2010 ANC National General Council, Durban

Index